Looking, Seeing and Knowing

Hunt Henion, PhD

Shift Awareness Books
for a Better Perspective!

Copyright © 2008 Hunt Henion

ISBN: 978-0-9822054-2-6
Library of Congress Control Number: 2008907800

Edited by Dr. Robert Dager and Dale Henion

Book design by Five Rainbows Services

Printed in the United States of America.

Shift Awareness Books
www.ShiftAwareness.com

Don Quixote
Looking, Seeing & Winning
the battle for a Great Perspective!

The Don Q Point of View by Hunt Henion
The true story of Don Quixote and his perspective
Available from Shift Awareness Books or a bookstore near you.

Looking for a way out?
Check out *The BIG Fake-out, the illusion of limits* by Hunt Henion
From Shift Awareness Books or your favorite online supplier.

Contents

Introduction

When we *look* at the world, sometimes we can *see* the way things are, but we hardly ever really *know* anything for sure.

Our bodies act and our emotions and minds react as Soul looks on.

Soul knows, but that knowledge normally filters down to our consciousness in such small doses that we don't even recognize it for what it is. We typically belittle it, ignore it, and then go back to looking and scrambling blindly for the rest of our lives just as if the salvation of knowledge didn't even exist.

The ancients told true stories of the magic that circulates under the skin of the Earth and permeates the air. People listened eagerly hoping to learn more about the mystical forces of the One and how to cooperate better with them. I told these stories myself from the steps of the pyramids in the Ohio Valley 50,000 years ago.

Over time, people began to shift their attention from cooperation to competition with each other. This caused them to look for new answers, and caused me to come down from the pyramid and walk among them. Gradually, my attention shifted from service to personal attainment to a desperate survival mode along with everyone else. New storytellers emerged who played "what if" games with their anxious audiences. Minds expanded with new possibilities, scattering attention to the four winds and even further away from the answer to the dilemma of our existence.

Blown by the winds of imagination and misconception for many millennia, we've drifted further and further from the ancient knowledge of ourselves and our one true source. Today, many people are turning back, looking for the true stories which faded into oblivion long ago. They want to know about the One Source of our being, and how to cooperate with it. Although these people may not be in the majority yet, their reversal of desire has literally changed the future of all mankind. It's put a new a fork in the road; some will go one way, and some will go the other. The choice (for everyone born before 1998, at which point earthlings stopped being born with 3-D contracts) will be to either break their life contract with the 3-D world, or break their connection with Mother Earth when she departs the three dimensional arena. Either way, everyone will have to use their divine Free Will like never before. In preparation for that, some are already beginning to use their Free Will in new ways.

We've all heard stories about how people have had a near death experience but were pulled back to Earth when they got a vision of how their contract in this life wasn't over yet. However, how many stories have you heard about someone whose contract actually was up but lived to tell about it? What a miracle and blessing! Or so you'd think. Living past our contracted end will be easier someday. Eventually our evolution will make our desires manifest quicker. At that time, precontracted lives with their dependable parameters will probably become a thing of the past. However, for now, we're in a fairly awkward growing phase. As one of the first to cross this new threshold, I'm here to tell you that it's not easy! When life winds down (in accordance with prelife plans you made but are totally unaware of) despite your best efforts to reverse things, it's very depressing! Hitting that wall that was designated as your end is devastating. Changing direction, then rebuilding momentum is nearly impossible. And surviving the void between lives while actually living on Earth is a nightmare I wouldn't wish on anyone.

Yet, now that my life is suddenly in gear, I thought that I should retrace the miracles that carried me through those phases. I'll start with some of my history before entering this lifetime to illustrate my motivation. I'll tell you about the life contract process as I know it, and illustrate how breaking that contract can work. My multi-life story, combined with some observations on the history of the world, should help reinforce what you already know in your heart. I'll relate what I see, then you decide if this adds to the reality you know or not. To many my version of life may seem too fantastic to be real. I might not even have believed it myself a while back. Yet, things are changing fast now. **My purpose in writing this is to help bring the reader up to speed before "the end of time," and inspire confidence in the power of our own abilities—even as we all listen to the drums of chaos in the night between now and then.** There's *one* little *thing* that I especially hope everyone will come to know better. It usually gets overlooked as we negotiate our way through life's successes and failures, and is often only realized after most of life's important decisions are behind us. It may be the sign of an advanced soul to see that situation as humorous, but the joke of not knowing what we need to know before it's too late is getting a little old. Like everyone, I've been too busy with my own agenda to see the simple answer that has been staring me in the face my entire life. When my life was over, though I still walked on the Earth, I somehow began to see everything much clearer. As I looked at everything, *one thing* suddenly became more important than everything else! EVERYTHING is still really compelling. My own developing story and the unfolding drama of mankind is tremendously captivating! Still, it's all about *one* very common, well-known little *thing*. I'd tell you right now what that is, but then you wouldn't appreciate it anymore than you do already. It has to be presented just right. That's what life is all about, and that's the goal of *Looking, Seeing & Knowing*.

The urge to fight manifested as a life among those who stormed the Russian Palace (during the Bolshevik Revolution)...concurrent with this life as a Russian, my higher self simultaneously manifested another body as a man who became a hermit in the Yucatan.

1

Business as Usual

I was born during the last decade of the 1800s with the angry urge to change society as well as the desire to leave it. These two motivations manifested two different bodies in two separate sections of the world, about 20 years before the beginnings of the Bolshevik revolution. I ran two totally separate lives on two completely different paths—both ending with a very similar moral which led to my reluctance to come back to Earth again.

The urge to fight manifested as a life among those who stormed the Russian palace in St. Petersburg as an outcry against the injustices of the Czar. I was unaware at the time that Dowager Empress, Marie Feodorovna Romanova, the grandmother of Anastasia, was working behind the scenes for the same reforms in Russia that I wanted to initiate. I was also unaware that this woman, whom I assumed was my archenemy, was actually a close member of my soul family and was to become my beloved daughter, Veda, born in 1996.

Maybe her efforts would have worked a lot better than mine. I died young, and my poor worried mother from that lifetime still looks over me today. From the afterlife, I saw the temporary government I helped put into power quickly topple, giving way to a new experimental, socialistic government which struggled its way to a slow death. I saw that all my efforts and sacrifice had failed to bring the masses any of the benefits which had been promised. Some benefited from the chaos, but most didn't. If I had realized that I fought against a well-meaning member of my soul group, I would have been even more discouraged when I died than I already was.

Previous lives had already discouraged me enough so that concurrent with this lifetime as a Russian, my higher self simultaneously manifested another body as a man who became a hermit in the Yucatan. It wasn't a bad life at all, and that embodiment of me lived a lot longer.

In that incarnation, I gave up my previous devotion to helping improve the human condition. The more I withdrew from active participation in the world, the more I felt assaulted by the thoughts attitudes of others. I retreated to the jungles whenever I could. After I finished building a little hut, I only returned to civilization for provisions.

Then, I stopped even doing that as I learned to provide for myself. I grew very comfortable in the company of the spirits around me. I also became resolved to my resentment when I had to actually acknowledge another human in my neck of woods, with their intrusive thoughts and attitudes.

By now, the Dowager Empress Marie had died and was reborn to a woman in Mexico who had been my wife back in ancient Egypt. Veda (not her name in that lifetime), who had been the Dowager Empress, was born in Mexico in the early1930s and contacted me psychically in my hermitage when she was about twelve. Veda would channel me to her mom, and I'd tell them both about the beauty of my life under the canopy of the jungle.

This continued for several years until WW II broke out. Then one day, Veda went on a mission of mercy and got a knee injury. It got infected and she died well before I ever did. That was a blow to both her mother and me.

At that point, I lost communication with her mom. Then I found out just a while ago, that when she died, she went to live in the forest as a wood nymph basically looking for the beauty I had told her about, and to some degree, looking for me. She contacted Veda just a year ago, and as far as I know she's still there. Attracted to the forest life like her mom, after I vicariously shared that experience with them both, Veda was reborn as a fairy after she died in the 1940s. However, she was a little heavy for that world and didn't stay long.

When I ended both of my virtually simultaneous lives (as a Russian and a hermit in the Yucatan), I was very discouraged with life and felt at a loss of what to do to make it better for myself and those I loved. Yet, after some healing in heaven, an opportunity presented itself, and I became suddenly anxious to experience life on Earth one more time.

Still, it's hard to argue with your higher self when you know he knows best. His final word on the subject was something like, "Well, you know it's not supposed to be heaven."

2

<u>Signing My Life Away</u>

I was just hanging out, talking to a few friends and enjoying eternal bliss when I saw a man circulating around the crowd. When I wondered what he was doing, I suddenly knew—which is that way things work in heaven. He was looking for people with a specific "unique energy" to volunteer for a mission on Earth. I didn't know exactly what that mission was, and he didn't really know what was going to be happening with the earth. Still, he needed volunteers to help on an energetic basis, and I was hoping he'd ask me.

Sure enough, he found his way to our little group and asked if I'd consider going back to Earth to help with the planetary ascension. When he said he was looking for people to place strategically around the physical world, my buddies were quick to offer their counsel: "Are you crazy?"

"Don't you remember what it was like…?"

Brushing off their comments and questions, I eagerly agreed to go.

This man who had gotten me moving again made his simple logistics requirements known to my higher self who I knew would meet me in the life contract meeting room. At the beginning of the day, going back to Earth was the last thing on my mind. Yet, here I was, looking forward to it.

Picture a long line outside a little bungalow at the edge of heaven. I stood there in line I don't know how long, talking to those around me.

I wasn't really in any hurry and the people around me were pretty interesting. There wasn't a very strict order to the line and people were milling around working their way ahead of me. A few anxious ones were trying to get through to the front of the line as quickly as possible. No one seemed to mind. Then, there were a few going the other direction too. Guess they needed more time to figure out what they wanted.

I didn't think I had that problem. Still, as I started to ponder what I wanted out of my next life, a simple definitive answer didn't really occur to me. Visions of my past choices began to play out like a movie in my mind.

Although my hermitage in the Yucatan was a happy, full life as I joyfully connected to the spiritual entities and realities around me, I knew I was missing something because of the lack of human interaction. Yet, there were a string of other lives full of seemingly fruitless interactions and conflicts. I had just stepped out of one of those lives where I fought in the Russian Revolution. The outcome was very disappointing, and I wasn't anxious to trust my human perception about such things again.

These memories of missions and conflicts, where I felt devoted to what I clearly felt was a righteous cause, filled my mind. I saw how my lives touched others and the good I did. I also saw where my best efforts failed to make the difference I wanted. Detached from human emotions, I pondered this utter lack of success. The quandary of how to best deal with the human dilemma still perplexed me.

I had recovered from the emotional trauma, or I wouldn't have been in line. Still, I wasn't anxious to repeat any of my mistakes, and I had made so many! In just my last lifetime, I had been very involved in the world in one body, and had totally escaped involvement with another. Both were disappointing. This left me wondering about a possible alternative.

Sure, I wanted to go back. I had a mission now, and the chance to make some personal progress was appealing. Still, I didn't know what I wanted to do. I certainly didn't want to get seriously committed again and make another big mistake. I wanted to get more involved than the hermit, but not so caught up in things that the Universe would be triggered to teach me the humility lesson again. These were the concerns, which flitted through my mind as I made small talk with the others in line around me.

Before long I felt really close to those people I hardly even knew. Since they weren't family, I knew I might not see them again for a very long time, if ever. Still, as I prepared for my turn to go into the contract room, human feelings of missing these new friends never even crossed my mind. The feeling of being always close to everyone was an ever-present premise. It was just one of those perks of the place I was about to leave which didn't really occur to me I was giving up.

When I stepped into the room full of many familiar and some not so familiar faces, I saw a simple wooden table with four chairs around it. All the members of the family I was about to enter into physically were there. My higher self explained that he had chosen parents for the genetic, karmic, and environmental characteristics they would bring to my life. A special mix of the genes provided by these two parents would determine my physical, emotional, and mental reactions. I remember a discussion about a few of the components, which weren't really what I would have picked.

Still, it's hard to argue with your higher self when you know he knows best. His final word on the subject was something like, "Well, you know it's not supposed to be heaven."

What could I say to that? My higher self and I were the first to sit down to the table. We shared a vision of my past and future lives and agreed on where the one coming up fit. We both took this all in, but as usual, I had the most say about the physical and motivational particulars of my life based on my recent life experiences and how I currently saw things. My higher self never cares much. He can take any situation and twist it around so I learn what I need to.

It seemed to me that on that fateful day, my main input was that I didn't want to get involved like I had before. Since I really didn't know what I wanted, and because I had reservations about the whole earthly experience thing, I didn't want to stay around very long. Thinking about the disappointments of thousands of lifetimes, I finally said, "I know I agreed to go back, but I'd like to reenter the world on sort of a trial basis. I don't really want to stay any longer than I have to."

Then, thinking about that life as a hermit, I said, "I probably need to work my way slowly back into civilization, but I know I could take at least one lifetime getting that right."

Then I added, "As long as I'm going, I would like to make some personal progress in learning to live more comfortably among people without fighting the way things are or isolating myself."

Before I could elaborate on my list of three incompatible requests, he said, "Done; done and done."

My higher self is a man of few words, and he works in mysterious ways. I was still trying to figure out how to reconcile all my diverse requests when the words appeared on the contract page in front of me. I didn't read all the small print, but the gist of it was that I would be born first into a transitional life as a Russia who would work in the forests. He wouldn't ever be involved with people much, but he would start getting me acclimated to the world of people again in a peaceful way.

About 20 years later, I'd be born to a middle class family in America. I'd marry and lead a relatively normal, middle class existence. That entire life (which carried lots of apprehension for me) would last until I was about 52, ending before all the messiness of old age. Approximately 20 years into that life, a third person would be born, and I'd run another simultaneous life in India. She would really get a grip on this business of living a happy and productive life among humans. She wouldn't give up her psychic abilities, but they wouldn't drive her into isolation either. The first life would help me transition into the second which would help me transition into the third.

All three of these manifestations of me were to be placed in the far corners of the world, which worked well with my original purpose of being one (in this case three) of the people strategically placed around the world to help with the Earth's ascension. It also seemed to accomplish what I'd personally asked for, so I agreed. The rest of what I recall only relates to the middle manifestation of my soul. I only have a general understanding of the particular contract arrangements of my other two embodiments.

As for the memories of the middle me, I recall that Phyllis, my first wife, was there. We sat down at the table and came to terms with our future relationship. The probable future of our highs and lows, bonds and conflicts, giving and taking, were all planned out, and we arrived easily at an amicable agreement.

Next I sat down with (let's call her) Joy, a woman who was to be my second wife. My life with her was to be representative of that incarnation. When I was a kid, I couldn't wait to grow up and get married. I knew she was coming, and that was all I personally wanted out of that incarnation. Since I was opting for an early exit with few regrets, I wouldn't say our relationship was going to always be blissful, but it was going to be full of life, and it was something I understood and wanted. However, it never happened.

In retrospect, missing my connection with Joy was a major turning point in my life. It ended up leading to a chain of events, which prevented me from leaving this world on time. Then, the realization that my contract had expired without taking me with it was the trigger which inspired my search for the personal and universal answers which are all explored in this book.

Conspicuously missing from the contract room was Spencer, a member of my core family group, and my mother from my recent previous life in Russia. They had both signed on to be my constant inner companions. They weren't there because it didn't matter what I decided. They were precontracted to always be by my side because of their love bond for me. They are my spiritual touchstones and have become constant reminders in recent years of the presence of a loving universe no matter what I think I see happening in my life.

Before I knew it, all the contract issues had been accounted for. I had arranged for what I wanted, and my higher self had vowed to work with me to help turn my desires into the highest possible good for all concerned. I didn't know exactly know what that meant, but I didn't need to. Those sorts of administrative details are all handled by our higher selves, so that we can give our attention to the business of living.

I had forgotten how complex and dynamic the forces of life on Earth can become. It isn't that way anywhere else. I also had no way of knowing how I'd end up fighting the flow of things my contract had initiated in order to try to cooperate with my higher self when my time was about up. Still, as he said, "It's not supposed to be heaven." We had arranged what I asked for, and with that thought, I found myself leaving the room.

"Next!" was the last thing I heard as consciousness slipped away and I fell into the darkness. The contract was hardwired into my genes after I left the room, and the next thing I knew I was coming through the hospital ceiling, looking down at the painful trauma of my mama. I closed my eyes, and when I opened them, quicker than the voice from above could say, "Bob's your second dad," I found myself separated from the world I knew and at the mercy of a contract I could never entirely comprehend for what felt like an eternity.

These egotistical and rebellious genes are phase one of the mechanism. Our resulting reactions are phase two.

...They (guides) will lay out material for us to build with (such as setting up situations) much like a contractor would lay out materials after referring to a blueprint. That's phase three, or the third level of benefits, in the mechanism that helps us complete our life contracts.

3

Contract Benefits

Speaking as Hunt, the middle manifestation in my trinity consciousness, I'd say that one of my favorite benefits from this contract was the osmosis of consciousness that came from the Russian who learned to exist among people without running away or getting all worked up with the need to change the world. He feels like a fatherly presence, and his life is a comforting lesson. Now that I know of his existence, his experience and very familiar energy is even more accessible.

When I was younger, I had many experiences where I'd get a splinter and whine to the universe about how bad that felt. An inner voice would always say, "Just be glad you don't work with wood for a living." Then I'd hear lots of muffled laughter and snickering. After a while I got the idea that there was an inside joke, and I wasn't on the inside. After decades of this going on, I guess they got tired of the joke because it stopped happening. Now I finally get it.

However, before getting to know this strong and extremely interesting person, the benefits of my contract seemed to have worked against my conscious efforts most of my adult life. Every major event in my life, no matter how successful, carried the essence of the early demise I had requested. Things could only be so successful and still be in harmony with the plan to ease me out of the world with no regrets when my time came.

I had reservations at the contract table about the parents, family, and general upcoming childhood condition. There was uncomfortable karma with my mother, and my father had only agreed to stick around for less than ten years of my life. That one issue caused me great concern. I couldn't blame him for wanting out earlier than normal. Still, even before leaving the table, I was worried…

I understood that many of these things were designed to help me grow and learn. However, I also understood that many of them simply fell into the "nothing's perfect" category, and that was fine. Those things actually worked as a benefit toward the goals of my contract which meant that they helped me prepare for checking out of this world at the preassigned time.

The physical mechanisms that activate the terms of our contract are as interesting as the whole proposition of a contracted life template, which is what the contract process provides. Besides having genes for the color of our eyes and hair, we also have genes that determine our emotional reactions (i.e. flaws). These egotistical and rebellious genes are *phase one* of the mechanism. Our resulting reactions are *phase two*.

Because of human Free Will, we have a natural bent for rebellion. Our personal emotional reactions interact with the similarly volatile emotional nature of those around us that, in turn, feeds back into our reactions. This vicious cycle leads to escalating conflicts, a withdrawal from the world, a search for outside help, or all of the above.

If this outside help involves reaching out for divine intervention, those who respond to assist will simply refer to our life contract. They'll lay out material for us to build with (such as setting up situations) much like a contractor would after referring to a blueprint. That's *phase three,* or the third level of benefits, in the mechanism which helps us complete our life contracts.

When the project is built, the contract is over, and that provision is also often encoded in a gene, which will cause a fatal illness at the prescribed time. Thus, a termination gene often works with everything else to bring about the end of life at a generally agreed upon age. General opinion on what's normal feed this expectation. Yet in the end, it really is a life choice by the individual. This generally agreed upon life span is more finely tuned for each individual in the contract room and then affirmed or adjusted somewhat during our physical lives.

Until the project/life is complete, we'll keep getting help to complete it whether we want it or not. Our enlightened Free Will, which we used before coming here generally takes precedent over what the human self thinks it wants when in the physical vehicle. Convincing the Universe that our current desires are more appropriate than our original ones isn't a simple process. However, getting in touch with our higher self to renegotiate our contract can and does redefine the limits of our human Free Will. Our potential use of this power is awesome, but then so is the power illusion.

We ignorant humans always think our reactions are reasonable or at least a result of our Free Will. Actually what we think of as our "Free Will" reactions are generally just a result of our genetic programming. True, Free Will is a standard perk for human life contact. However, it's not generally what you might think. We assume a lot of things are our Free Will because we actually just don't understand the powers affecting us. Without going into tedious detail, I'll just say that many of these mysterious, personal powers within our bodies, minds and surroundings were prearranged in our life contracts.

The contract we make is like a track in an amusement park on which our little cars are born to run. As a kid, we sit in the passenger seat and pretty much just go along for the ride. As we grow into big kids, we learn to take the wheel. We make minor adjustments to direction using the steering wheel, but it generally doesn't really matter what we do or how we react. Our little cars are going to stay on the track we contracted to be built especially for us. We were working with divine clarity, all the major parties involved in our lives, and with the power of all the heavenly creative forces. So it's a good track, and usually the best thing we can do is to resign ourselves to just calmly stay the course.

Actually, our general human contract provides a genetic makeup that tends to push us to make a few choices, which might result in a detour or two. This is what we know as "Free Will." However, usually all paths within our realm of the choices we're inclined to make will eventually lead to the same contracted experiences, and end up in the same place and on schedule. You may bring a variety of lessons to the end of the track, but the main contracted experiences are covered by all the options—generally.

True, now and then, people do jump the track. This is usually a big mistake for themselves and everyone else around them. We'll talk a lot more about that later, but the point for now is that usually, people just make minor adjustments in their lives.

The change we initiate may feel major, but if it wasn't a precontracted change, the universe simply works it's magic to bring us back on course one way or another so our contract can be fulfilled. In other words, Free Will usually just takes us on detours, and one turn doesn't generally change our entire contract because of all of the forces at work to bring us back on course.

This may not seem like a lot of leeway, but it's much more than any other dualistic world has ever been trusted with, and it's more than enough to get us in a lot of trouble. Without Free Will, people are more naturally connected, and they flow along with things in a more natural order.

Our Free Will has usually been used to foster separation between us and source, and between us and everyone else. This has gotten us in trouble with the environment, socially, spiritually, and in every way possible. Now, that we've gotten ourselves into all this trouble with the little bit of Free Will that we've been allowed, what do you suppose should happen? Instead of taking it away, our Free Will is actually being muscled up through the thinning of the veil between our human and higher selves.

This is simply part of our recent, rapid evolution. Yet it feels like a big vote of confidence that we'll suddenly start to use our Free Will wisely to get ourselves out of all this trouble. Cool, huh?

This is actually an enhancement to the contract benefits we (all of us born before 1998 who had 3-D contracts) signed up for. It's a new perk to being born into this very special time.

Actually, there are some controls in place to help balance out the dynamics of extreme positive and negative uses of our new, more powerful Free Will. For instance, the benevolent forces that monitor Earth activity aren't allowing us to blow each other or the Earth up with atomic weapons anymore. Our space brothers are also nullifying man-made diseases before they can nullify all of us. So, with controls like this in place, our natural evolution which tunes us into a more enlightened use of Free Will and is leading to largely constructive uses.

Now, it seems I've become one of the test subjects of what our increase in Free Will can do. When I contracted for a short life, I didn't realize (no one did) that I might be able to change that plan by exercising a new option. I also didn't realize that my limited prearrangements would be biting me in the butt if I ever tried to do so.

Everything was going according to plan. As I mentioned, my dad was contracted to check out when I was nine. That was one of the first events that confirmed my desire to leave early too. When he passed away, that was the first blow to my enthusiasm which helped prepare me for my early departure from the earth plane.

The following summer, I had a body surfing accident in which I later discovered I had ruptured two disks in my neck. The pain from that accident grew over the years and provided a constant dampener on my hopes and expectations about life. Again, this was another benefit from my contract, which was preparing me for an early exit from the world.

There were many bright spots in my life, but since I signed up for an early out, the Universe was always gearing me up for that. I had some successes in school, scholastically and socially. My kids were a very big bright spot. However, now I can see how the consequences of my contract were always fighting my best efforts to make a strong, long range, positive plan for my life. The Universe was simply running the program I helped create so that I could leave early and without a lot of regrets.

Throughout it all, my higher self was seizing every opportunity to conspire against the odds to help me to jump track and break my contract. There were turning points in my life which I now see didn't proceed as planned. I used Free Will to change those plans, which was a good thing!

However, losing my contracted arrangements threw me into a depressing void where I had to try to operate without prearranged setups. Suddenly, I had no definite direction, and a loss of power caused by the general confusion from jumping the track. That was the first noticeable result from actually exercising my Free Will. There were bright spots, but things just seemed to go from bad to worse for quite a while.

Those depressing times increased the force that pushed me back toward my contracted path. Yet, I wasn't going back to that track! I continued to fight that flow of natural inclinations moving continually away from my contracted future. Everything felt so wrong for so long that a new motivation for life developed. I really wanted to live to see what was going on! Now, I realize that jumping track and enduring those difficult times is the only reason I'm alive and thriving today.

{ ...there is a lesson here for those of us who occasionally regret making what looks like mistakes: No matter how sure you are that you screwed up, and no matter how much that realization hurts, I'm here to tell you that you could be wrong—yet again. Thank God for mistakes! }

4

My Turning Points

Looking through that cloud of possibilities, I see two major alternative lives which were often more dear to me than the life I was actually living. They embodied my hopes and dreams, and in one case, the torment of missing my contracted love.

My first chance to do things differently than I did came in the beginning years of college. I lived on my own, supporting myself and paying for college expenses myself for most of my college career. Still, after the first year, I took my parents advice and switched from the humanities major, which I absolutely loved, to a business major, which contributed nicely to my contracted downward cycle.

I wasn't really strong enough to resist my parents' wisdom, so I never really considered the alternative life I kept seeing as a real missed opportunity. I kept telling myself it never could have happened. However, occasional images of the progress of that alternative life persisted, and channeled information has now confirmed the details of its existence.

It was a fairly perfect life for me. I was only marginally involved in the world behind the gates of academia, and I was doing what I loved most: writing and lecturing to a captive and admiring audience. However, now I realize that if I had been strong enough to make that choice, I also would have been strong enough to make a couple of other choices, which never even crossed my mind on the path I'm currently traveling.

Those choices led to my early demise, which I'm sure the Universe saw as consistent with my contract for an early departure.

Billy said that I didn't actually die on schedule in that life, but I did "die emotionally." He also said, "There's still hope for him."

This prompted me to ask if my renewed enthusiasm for life may be bleeding over to him. However, it seems it doesn't work that way. Alternative lives are normally pretty separate—except for the regret we tend to feel when we get glimpses of that greener looking grass.

The other alternative life, which was really my contacted life, ended in an early death, at about the age of 52. After my first divorce, back in my late 20s, when I asked about my future romance, I got a vision of what I thought was the perfect woman. Without going into details (which I did in *The BIG Fake-Out*), I'll just say that she was so perfect that I didn't believe the vision. I assumed I must have imagined it all.

After being flustered and faked-out by almost thirty years of physical existence, I totally missed the clues and rejected the premonition about her coming into my life. When I finally met her in the physical, I instantly recognized her from my premonition and realized what had happened. My heart almost stopped right then.

However, since I was already married (again), it was too late. She left town shortly after that, and she commented to a few of us that she was never really sure why she came to town in the first place. It's interesting how forces set in motion stay in motion even after we veer off in another direction. The forces of our contract brought her to town even though I was already married, and they moved me toward an early completion of my life even though, by not hooking up with her, I had changed that outcome.

At any rate, I did confront her one day after she moved away. I told her about my premonition of meeting her and my continued visions of our alternative life together. She took it rather well, but said that she never thought of me in any sort of a romantic way. That's probably as it should be, but then why did our paths have to cross?

Inertia—that's all I ever came up with. I had used Free Will to remove the possibility of romance with her, but conditions had already been set in motion for our meeting. Sometimes things work for mechanical reasons and looking for spiritual significance where there isn't any (unless we invent it) can drive a person crazy.

Channeling confirmed that she had been at the contract table help-ing me plan the brightest aspect in my otherwise short and dismal life. Maybe, my higher self hoped for a higher purpose for me, and helped me miss that appointment. I don't know...

All I know for sure is that for the next couple of decades, I was totally obsessed with missing my contracted love. My heart physically hurt most of the time, and I couldn't help checking in on that alternative life to see how it was going. I saw when we had a little girl. I saw her grow up. I saw the problems we had, and I saw us separate for a while. I was delighted when we got back together, and actually felt the humility and deep, grow-ing love that this alternative self had for this woman.

I tried to ignore that alternative life after that, but one day I realized that this couple which never existed in my reality, but whom I felt closer to than family, had gotten a divorce. That eased my anguish over this "mistake" some.

Then, I realized that in that reality, about six months later, I'd died—right on schedule. An aneurism took me quickly after I had cut the ties with my wife. Also, my daughter was in her late teens and self-possessed enough to do okay without me.

My first reaction was that my death must have been tied to a broken heart that blinded me from my options for life. It seemed obvious that my higher self quickly found a way to cure my discouragement and fulfill my contract after that. However, that's just part of the picture.

In retrospect, I can see the grand plan behind it all now. Despite my emotional reaction to the divorce, it was a good plan! Cutting the ties with my wife before I passed on was probably the most loving way to leave. My wife and daughter were eased out of the relationship that way, and it was gentlest on everyone.

This realization was prompted by seeing this alternative me being greeted like a returning hero on the other side. He was congratulated for things going so well while on Earth. During the difficult times I've had since then, that vision fills me with regret. I wondered for many years why I was still alive and why my own impatience was allowed to rob me of my contracted life (and then my escape from life). Yet, when I got a grip, I could see that my potential for a happy and use-ful life (after my contracted life was concluded) was becoming clearer all the time.

This potential started with some seeds I planted before that fork in the road. One was the desire to write, and I even saw the name of the book I would write some day. However, because that potential was in an alternative reality, I had no way to relate to it. Still, I tried, and that effort started moving me off my contracted path. The other desire, which wasn't part of my original plan, was to have my dad back. I saw him coming to me as my son, but that wasn't part of the original plan either. Yet, both these desires were realized on the path I moved into.

Assuming I'm not totally crazy, there is a lesson here for those of us who occasionally regret making what looks like mistakes: No matter how sure you are that you screwed up, and no matter how much that realization hurts, I'm here to tell you that you could be wrong—yet again. Thank God for mistakes!

The thing I see in common with those two missed opportunities (leading the life as the professor, and not marrying my contracted love) is that they both offered a degree of comfort which I never found (in the reality I know best), at lease not yet, which is well after my original life contract ended. As the man who continued the major in college he loved, I sailed through my schooling, enjoying the experience tremendously. I then hid behind the ivy-covered walls receiving recognition and never having to really deal with the world of layoffs, financial disaster, or the lack of any permanent structure in my life.

This was also true if I had married my contracted romance. I would have moved to an area which would have better supported my business until I died. In both cases, life would have been full and good. I would have fallen into a comfortable niche and not wanted out until my contracted time.

However, since I only had one contracted life, I only had one contracted end. Both the life I'm currently living and the alternative life as the professor simply felt the inclination to end life as that time came and went. We both got really depressed, and had to struggle to regroup after the scheduled demise was over. If something had happened which ended our lives, we would have fulfilled the contract. Yet nothing was set up for those alternative lives to accomplish that end.

It's all pretty interesting to stand back and look at. I never fell into any comfortable niche. I wished I was dead too early, and when my time finally came I was still scrambling to make things work. I didn't overpower my departure time with a conscious choice based on any awareness of a higher purpose. Nor did I miss my contracted life on purpose. All I know for sure is that I was out of synch with my preprogrammed destiny.

I strongly suspect that my higher self had a hand in throwing a wrench into the works. For instance, I saw this book, *Looking Seeing & Knowing,* with my name as author, in an astral library when I was in my early 20s—before I ever had a chance to miss my contracted romance, which would have locked me into a life that would have steered me away from ever writing this book. I never started writing until after my contracted departure time, and it was motivated by all the experiences I had after leaving my contracted path. I strongly suspect that my higher self heard my desire to write this book (and others), and started taking steps to provide for that option.

My turning points came and went without my conscious awareness. Yet my higher self seems to have had a grasp on the options pretty early. When I asked if I'd ever write anything that got published, he simply showed me this book. He didn't say what conditions would be required to realize that reality. Still, that's probably when I started coming into harmony with the alternative life I'm currently living.

Life has felt like one mistake after another ever since I missed that "fork in the road" romance. Of course one "mistake" leads to another, and the more we scramble with a hope and a prayer to make things work, the more our higher selves have a chance to work their magic in setting up a new order. The woman I married instead of waiting for my contracted love gave me a son. She had a daughter from a previous marriage whom I dearly love, but our son saved my life. Dale (my son whom I named after my father—because he was the reincarnation of my father) was another turning point. The desire to have him back in my life was a seed that grew into a deep appreciation for the path I inadvertently took.

However, that appreciation didn't occur over night. Life was nose-diving nicely, right on schedule, when my son came along and started healing my wounds and giving me a new purpose for being. I may not even have made it to my contracted age of expiration if it hadn't had been for him.

Another turning point in the positive direction came after being laid off from my job as a business forms "dealer consultant," when I hit on an idea for a business. I designed a form that went over pretty well. I built a business around that form, and that also probably saved my life.

It actually made money after trying numerous things for a few years that failed miserably. It also allowed me to work at home, which later became a big advantage for the raising of kids.

While I was married to Dale's mom, we fell into a health-conscious crowd. I did all sorts of cleansing regimens which evidently reversed my predisposition to the aneurism, which killed me in the alternative life. I was the same person up to that point in the road. However, marrying the "wrong" woman led to a different life style that saved my life.

Other than that, the marriage to Dale's mom went fairly badly, as did the next one. However, the next one also renewed my lease on life by giving me two daughters. This woman also had a daughter I love as much as my own. However, I recognize my two little girls (and being granted primary custody of them) as primary turning points in my life.

Veda is from my core soul family group, and similarities between us are downright scary. Noel was sent here to help me. I got that message the day she was born.

I was told Noel came originally from the dolphin world, and true to that playful and enlightened spirit, she's helped both Veda and me lighten up and enjoy life. Billy said that when I get really serious and heavy, my energy changes and I can't do the job I was sent here to do. Noel helps with that.

At any rate, I now see these two little blessings, which gave me a reason to hang on a little longer, as a major turning point. They inspired the sense of responsibility that helped me hang on through my contracted end. It was a really close call though. I was told that during channeling and I knew it anyway. I was really ready to leave this world for several years.

My 52nd year in particular was probably my biggest turning point. During that year, when Veda was in the 5th grade, she would always worry that she'd come home to find me dead. Dale tells me that he was concerned about the same thing at about the same time. There were many days I had to go over my list of reasons for not just checking myself out. I was probably also really vulnerable to accidents during those times. Maybe it was my higher self pulling strings, but somehow no piano ever fell out of the sky on me.

For one reason or another, I managed to keep on kicking until my contract expiration had come and past. That's when my life had a real turning point!

Suddenly, without a contract that was conspiring with the forces of the universe to ease my way out of this world, I finally found that my hopes and prayers for a new beginning could be answered. Suddenly all the theories of self-actualization and the ability to manifest the realities I wanted, which I had been fighting the flow to believe in all my adult life, began to feel like real possibilities.

I had been surfing a particular online personals service for the better part of six years. So had Danna, but her guides were protecting her from me because, as far as anyone (almost anyone) knew, I was slated for recycling. However, after that probability passed, we met and have been living happily ever after ever since.

Billy said I was like the Phoenix who rose from the ashes of my former life. It was literally like being resurrected from a living death. At first, walking around with no contract felt like being dead to the world. Then, I began to realize that I was very much alive in a world where most people are deadened by their simple, precontracted plans. That stirred additional contempt in me until I discovered the beginnings of my own simple plan—a nice little niche surrounded by loved ones, enjoying the creative task of mapping this uncharted territory in which I've suddenly found myself.

...this new uncharted territory
didn't just stretch out in front of
my ended earthly contract. It also
manifested whenever I used Free
Will to break out of the stipulations
of the contract...Still, what is that
standard contractual language?
"Voiding one clause of the contract
does not automatically void any of
the other clauses."

In other words, even though the
life I was supposed to lead up to
the termination date was null and
void, that termination date was still
a black hole that pulled everything
I tried to do down into it.

5

Uncharted Territory

I shall be telling this with a sigh somewhere ages and ages hence:
Two roads diverged in a wood, and I—I took the one less traveled by,
And that has made all the difference.

—Robert Frost

Missing your exit appointment from life is more than simply taking the path "less traveled." It's more like suddenly finding yourself lost in the middle of the wilderness with no map and not even a faint deer trail to follow. Not only was there no path in front of me, but there was no way back either!

When I discovered that I was in uncharted territory and that my life contract had actually ended a couple years ago, I had lots of questions. "How was I supposed to have died? What was the turning point? If I had died a couple years ago, wouldn't my life have been fairly pointless? Can you tell me about how my life would have gone and how it would have affected the people in my life if I had died? Is a new contract set up yet?"

I asked all those questions in channeling and more, and the only one Billy actually answered was the last one: "No. You don't have a contract anymore. Your life is what you make of it now."

I'd heard that "life is what you make of it," before. However, now that I was finally no longer fighting myself and the inclinations motivated by my old contract, I was just beginning to learn how true that saying could be. On the other hand, I really didn't have much of a direction or much to work with. The universe had removed my most of my baggage such as career and wife, hope and joy…in preparation for departing this world.

During that first channeling session, when I was told that I was in new uncharted territory, I was really anxious to know more about what was going on. Billy said to "Keep your eye on the big picture. If you pull at any of the loose strings, the whole thing might unravel."

Billy seems like a regular guy most of the time, but once in a while he says some really profound things. I was just beginning to create a new contract with my assumptions and hopes. Looking at reality too closely sometimes can reveal little reason for our expectations.

If you pull at a string of thoughts too hard, you may miss the big picture because of the close up appearance of things. I've gotten a serious appreciation lately for how illusion can protect us from realizing realities, which would otherwise be so daunting that we'd never challenge them. So, all in all, it's better not to push for too much understanding because who knows what that could undo.

Good advice, but pushing for understanding of all sorts of things is kind of what I do, and I couldn't help wondering about some of my other questions. For instance, "Wouldn't my life have been fairly pointless if I died on schedule?"

Billy had told me that my kids wouldn't have been as well off. This makes me think that my higher self was gambling their well being by giving them to me as motivation to stick around. That does speak to the usefulness of staying around but it doesn't really answer the question about the pointlessness of my life if I had left on time. Maybe I expect too much out of life, and the pointlessness of it all is the reason many end their lives. However, with me, finding out what was going on in this seemingly pointless life was a major reason for not ending it all.

When I asked my inner guides about the pointlessness of my life, the memory of something my higher self said came back to me, and seemed to echo in my head: "Done; done, and done."

Evidently, that's one reason for the three manifestations. Besides each fulfilling a different desire I had going to the contract table, this way, they had my Earth mission covered, even if the middle me veered from the contracted path and got temporarily lost or even died in the uncharted territory. For that matter, the middle manifestation of me is the only life that was blessed with an early-out clause. The others were strategically placed and holding the energy really well. The girl in India is a consistent dynamo of unique energy, and the man in Russia, who would be about 75 at this writing, is still going strong.

So even if I had fulfilled my contract by dying after I departed from the prearranged path, and even if my individual life was pointless (which no guide would ever admit), they still had my bigger purpose covered by the other manifestations of me. Actually, I think my alternative lives count for holding that energy too. They really happened somehow on some level on this same Earth. So, all in all, the planners would have gotten at least what they bargained for when they sent me down here, even if this middle manifestation of me did check out on schedule, regardless if I was on my contracted path or not.

As it turned out, the feeling of pointlessness was only temporary while I worked with my higher self to plot my new path. Shortly after that, Billy confirmed that I did have a life contract now. It was a relief when I first heard that I didn't have one anymore, but it was an even greater relief when I heard that I had a new track to run on. Too much control is a scary thing, and not having a plan is like not having a purpose in life.

Still, with very few temporary exceptions, everyone has a purpose and a contracted plan. Life can be difficult, frustrating, or even infuriating. Yet, as long as we're doing our best, it's never really pointless—no matter how things look.

As I write about living in the uncharted territory without a prearranged contract, I realize that this writing itself is going into uncharted philosophical territory. I've studied the popular gurus all my life. Still, these days, I find myself thinking about things I've never read or heard anyone else speak about: the power and limits of our life contracts, the fallacy of Free Will and the positive and negative use of the real thing;

the story of how we got Free Will (I'll get to that soon), the purpose of simultaneous physical manifestations of one person; dramatic, real reactions to alternative lives…

I'm intimately familiar with these debatable realities, and yet when I was working without the safety net of a life contract, no one on either side of the great divide really knew what I was going to make of all of this. That was exciting—to be on an equal footing with those on the other side who live without the obligatory contracted vow of ignorance we all take when coming to Earth.

At any rate, this new uncharted territory didn't just stretch out in front of my ended earthly contract. It also manifested whenever I used Free Will to break out of the stipulations of the contract. When I missed my contracted love arrangement, my whole life from then on took a detour from my contracted path. Still, what is that standard contractual language? "Voiding one clause of the contract does not automatically void any of the other clauses."

In other words, even though the life I was supposed to lead up to the termination date was null and void, that termination date was still a black hole that pulled everything I tried to do down into it. When the forces of the universe knew it was time for me to start winding down my career in preparation of my departure date, I was laid off and I absolutely couldn't get a job!

It didn't matter that I now had to make a living for the perceivable future. Jobs I thought I should get easily never even resulted in an interview. I was walking in uncharted territory where everyone had contracts except me, so as far as I can tell, I must have been invisible to them!

Originally, I had planned an entire chapter relating my experience navigating through and barely "Surviving the Void." However, like all those depressing "Contract Benefits" which I tried to skip over quickly, going too deeply into my experiences in the void (i.e. HELL) can get to be a downer pretty quickly.

I've gotten answers about all those questions I asked during that session when Billy warned me against pulling too much at the loose strings. Suffice it to say, I pulled carefully and reverently. I discovered many details about my own life, and I've come to an intimate understanding of how life contracts work.

I've come to see the life most people assume to be a wide-open universe of possibilities as a little egg around the soul which nurtures it with contracted agreements. This shell protects the growing soul from the world of chaos and generally non-productive possibilities. It makes a full, constructive life attainable by all. However, I also know now that it's possible to break out of that shell and into a whole new realm of possibilities!

As I sit here, still wet from being newly hatched from my egg of smothering influences, wondering where to start; there is only *One Thing* which comes to mind.

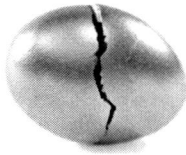

6

Breaking the Egg

Mine was the strangest birth under the sun; I left the womb,
yet life had not begun; entered the world, and yet was seen
by none.

—The Philosopher's Egg Riddle

According to legend, "the philosopher's egg" was the name given to the vessel in which alchemists hoped to produce the "philosopher's stone," an inexpensive material that could change the properties of anything. This vessel, which was constructed to hold the precious philosophers stone, was shaped as an egg for symbolic reasons. Ancient wisdom held that with this common material, you could transform anything into whatever you wanted. Hearing this, many throughout the ages have ambitiously tried to physically turn lead into gold. Yet in all that time, the identity of the *one thing* has remained a mystery.

When I finally broke out of the protective shell, which held me to conditions I no longer desired, I found myself landing in a world where others had contracts. Since I didn't, I really was often "seen by none." I sat there for a while wondering why nothing worked for me and why I was still walking around in this world. I moved about as unseen as the *one thing* which was necessary to bring order back into my life.

Actually, as a former hermit, "being seen by none" works pretty well for me. Also, in my after-contract life, my creation could finally be the result of my own conscious efforts instead of being led by pre-arranged conditions. I experienced this after the major turning points in my life too. After I missed those set up arrangements, I'd be in an uncharted territory just like when my planned life contract had run its course. I may have been invisible to many for a long time, but at least I wasn't fighting an invisible enemy anymore. The conditions I was unaware of setting up, over half a century ago before entering this world, finally weren't bothering me after my contract was over.

The big question was what to do now. What am I supposed to build my new life out of, and where do I start now that all the blueprints have been burnt? A quick magical answer would sure be nice.

What is the Philosopher's Stone and what's that Philosopher's Egg Riddle all about? What is it that breathes life into an object after its birth? What is it that brings a thing into manifestation so that it can be seen by all? What is the magical yet common element, which is the essence of all beginnings and transformations?

As with all questions I can verbalize, I got an answer. However before I just blurt it out, I want to point out that the answer explains how the phoenix is reborn from the ashes. It's why all that is worthwhile and needed in the world can be created out of something that's so common that it's been overlooked and constantly disregarded by modern man. Here's that same riddle expressed another way:

> The key to life and death is everywhere to be found,
> but if you do not find it in your own house, you will
> find it nowhere. Yet, it is before everyone's eyes; no
> one can live without it; everyone has used it. The
> poor usually possess more of it than the rich; children
> play with it in the streets. The meek and uneducated
> esteem it highly, but the privileged and learned
> often throw it away. When rejected, it lies dormant
> in the bowels of the earth. It is the only thing from
> which the Philosopher's Stone can be prepared, and
> without it, no noble metal can ever be created.

Any guesses? The above statement is full of cryptic hints:

1. This answer is the key that unlocks the door to all creat ion: health, wealth, enlightenment, and even immortality, or so they say. Yet this invaluable substance is "everywhere to be found."

   Mud is found everywhere and supposedly it's the stuff out of which they say God created us. Yet we might want to think along the lines of something as common as dirt but a bit more magical. What were we really created out of? You might want to read ahead in chapter 16 to answer that question, but unless you already know what the *one thing* is, that hint will probably just prolong the suspense.

2. The *one thing* is something that can only be discovered and understood by first going within our own "house." That must refer to our body, mind, spirit, heart or something like that.

3. People who blindly follow socially accepted values and beliefs have separated themselves from this thing by their misunderstanding of it. In this misunderstanding they don't' value it and "throw it away." Somehow, as society has evolved in its goals and priorities, quality and this elusive essential have gotten left out of the mix. Medieval alchemists frequently referred to this magical ingredient as "the Cornerstone the builders forgot."

4. The answer is "the only thing from which the Philosopher's Stone can be prepared." The Egyptian father of alchemy, Hermes Trismegistus, called this magical element the "*One Thing*" and wrote about it in his renowned Emerald Tablet. This tablet became the foundation of alchemical philosophy. This is what he wrote:

   > *That which is Below corresponds to that which is Above, and that which is Above corresponds to that which is Below, to accomplish the miracles of the One Thing. And just as all things come from this One Thing, through the meditation of One Mind, so do all created things come from this One Thing through Transformation. Its father is the Sun; its mother the Moon. The Wind carries it in its belly. Its nurse is the Earth.*

This is the original source of the quote "as above so below" which is often cited. This writing is also what motivated many men of the dark ages to become obsessed with literally turning lead into gold. They missed the real message here and so did the multitudes of wanabe magicians who came after them.

The alchemical gold is that *One Thing* which is within our being. It's forged in the fires of experience of this world. Then it's tempered in the tests of success and failure, as we experiment in applying this *One Thing* in our lives.

What makes a secret teaching a secret is not that it's never taught, but the fact that it's rarely caught. Blinded by their materialistic priorities, the experimenters in alchemy in the dark ages missed the real treasure of the "miracle" of "transformation" Hermes was trying to explain. They failed to grasp the true nature of the magical *One Thing*.

More hints probably won't help much, but I think its omnipotence and omnipresence deserves a little more introduction: The *One Thing* is what ignites life back into the ashes from which the phoenix is reborn. It's what creates everything, and is the *thing* out of which everything is created. Because it's the essence of everything, everything is It in disguise. Everything we do is an effort to get to know this *One Thing* better, so we can get to know ourselves, our origins, and our futures better.

As I sit here, still wet from being newly hatched from my egg of smothering influences, wondering where to start; there is only *One Thing* that comes to mind. It doesn't bother me a bit that those around me, living within the security of their contracted hits and scores, can't teach me the lost art of this magical element. Even the teachers who proclaim life's answers are generally doing so from a platform built in heaven. Very few have actually been stranded in life without any prearranged contacts and situations. So what do they really understand about the motivation for making that transition, let alone how to do it?

That's okay. I don't think I'd trust anyone to teach me about the lost art of alchemy anyway. Besides, changing the order of things feels a lot like playing with fire. We probably shouldn't unless we have to.

Personally, I have to since my preordained order ran out a few years back. I had a very disturbing dream the other night where I was on a huge houseboat with my kids. After a nice little ride, we were about to go over the edge of a huge waterfall. I shouted to those standing by, asking where the anchor was. No one knew. I asked for help turning the boat around. Again no one could help me.

I woke up wishing I had taken the detour out of this life so I wouldn't be facing going over the edge right now. That's when my lessons started.

I complained to the Universe about how unfair and harsh life was. A guide answered back, "That's why you learned to use magic."

Without disputing my feelings about the randomness of life, which I was not open to hearing, he simply said, "Now that you know the reason for exercising control over life, don't look back at that anymore. Look only to your own creation." Then he continued, "You wouldn't want to use the powers to change the course of a war," (which I did in a previous life) "but you can use it to clean up your own life and keep it positive."

So, my lessons in alchemy began again. He said that controlled thoughts and words would change my life all by themselves. He said this alone would take me out of the reactive cycle, which is the main source of the heavy karma for most people.

I remember learning this many times before, but I've always been sucked back into accepting the commonly believed precepts about life. I've justified this with ideas of fitting into society better. I've also consciously tried to lower my vibrations and ignore what I know for that same reason.

Recently, I was advised that, "It's time to stop that." Othello, the being my wife was channeling at the time, said that now's the time to connect with the Earth and my source no matter what others do. He said not to worry, and that others will follow.

Other advice was to keep my home and affairs clean and orderly if I wanted my life to have order. This guide told me to believe in the desires of my heart more than what my physical eyes see. He's helped me see myself and the philosopher's stone as the strong and stable force in the Universe. Like a black hole, I sit with my power in the center of my universe, bending what looks like reality to everyone else. Everything in that universe is fluid except the One Thing, which I know as the core of my heart.

This One Thing is the secret. It's not a tool to use as those in the dark ages thought. It is the ONLY thing, and as such we're all part of it. Using it is a mystical process that allows It to use us too. When we stand above it and use it to fulfill our every desire, no matter how worthy we believe our desires to be, the magic only works as long as it serves the karma generating purposes of the negative force. Then, disillusion sets in, and another hard-won lesson about human ego eventually emerges.

We can only consciously know so much. Then, as the ancient mapmakers used to say about the unexplored regions, "Beyond this lie dragons."

The further we venture away from our home and union with the *One Thing*, the more dangerous life becomes. It's our nature to explore, but when we find a patient union with the unknowable mind of the one thing, we've found home and THE most powerful seat from which see the world.

Lessons like this continued for several days. During that time, my guide told me not to need anything, because with need comes fear of not getting what we need. "See love in all things and all people. Take what you need from that."

As far as getting the answers we need to build confidence in life, he said, "All your questions and answers go hand in hand just outside the protective shell of ignorance which surrounds you. Asking questions expectantly from where you stand pokes holes in that shell so you can *look* through it. Similarly, your confidence in what you *see* can poke a hole in the egg of randomness around your life. What you come to *know* creates a new path in front of you."

He's assured me that I can come to learn all I need to about this lost art, just as anyone can. If we care enough to listen and take to heart what we learn, peace and harmony with the *One Thing* is guaranteed. The door to learning the proper use of the philosopher's stone is always open. All we have to do to leave the land of the dragons is to walk through it.

7

The Lost Art

As a man who has devoted his whole life to the most clear headed science to the study of matter, I can tell you as the result of my research about the atoms this much: "There is no matter as such!" All matter originates and exists only by virtue of a force, which brings the particles of an atom to vibration and holds this most minute solar system of the atom together... We must assume behind this force the existence of a conscious and intelligent mind. This mind is the matrix of all matter.
—Renowned scientist, Max Planck, during his acceptance speech for the Nobel Peace Prize

Notice the reference in the quote above to the holographic nature of the universe as Max compares an atom to a solar system. This is a man who used cold, hard science to back his way into an understanding of the ancient alchemic principle: *That which is below corresponds to that which is above, and that which is above corresponds to that which is Below, to accomplish the miracles of the One Thing.*

If there is "no matter as such," then what is there? What is the *One Thing*, consciousness? Actually, until you put consciousness in motion, you haven't really got any *thing* to be conscious of. Some *thing*, the *One*

Thing, is necessary to slant awareness toward intent and move consciousness into action.

In order to understand the "Intelligent mind" to which Max Planck refers, you need to understand its first manifestation: Nature, that living *matrix* which molds all creation. According to Webster, a matrix is "the womb; the cavity where anything is formed; a mold." The "intelligent mind" of the Universe uses the "womb" of Nature to create every*thing* from the *one* essential element which is at its heart. This *one* essential *thing* at its heart lends intent to the consciousness of Nature.

You could take the higher ground and say that the name of the *One Thing* at the heart of that matrix, "the womb or cavity where anything is formed," is Love. Alchemists generally take the practical approach by citing Harmony as the essential nature the *One Thing*. The concept of *harmony* tends to give the practitioner a little more leeway in its application than the purer concept of working with *love*. However, either way, whether the essential element required for creation is *love* or *harmony*, the fact remains that the understanding and use of these principles is a lost art.

Pythagoras taught that anything can be created simply by coming into harmony with it. You'd have to break down lead at the molecular level and rearrange the protons, neutrons and electrons until it resonated like gold to create gold, but with the science of harmony it is possible. Anything is possible.

Similarly, if we can learn to break down our egos to the essence behind them, we can fine-tune our vibrations until we come into harmony with anything we want to bring into our lives. All we need is The One basic element—love. Love is the dust out of which the soul of man was created. It's the breath of life. It's the binding force which attracts all with which we are in harmony.

Ever since we first took on selfish goals and priorities 5000 years ago in Babylon and built that temple to ego, we've been laboring under the illusion that the only essential thing is our own desires and will power. This has made the *one* real *thing* invisible to us. It "...entered the world but was seen by none." We've been living with the philosopher's stone in our hand all along, but have been trying to create without it!

However, an appreciation for the art of love and harmony has been growing as the rewards of ego have been declining recently. This seems to have started around 1850. Tremendous strides in conscious were made for about 60 years. Then enlightenment went into retreat again with WW I, and took a deep dive during WW II, only to emerge from its hiding place in the 1960s.

Even though materialism has taken its toll over the last couple decades, the increase of love and harmony has been a runaway freight train that no one can stop, as hard as they try. It may be hidden for the most part, but then that's the way of new power. It's born in secret and silence.

The illusion of national and world egos prospering at the expense of weaker societies has held up so far. Still, political revelations and Earth changes are gently opening our minds to new priorities, and those nudges are becoming less and less gentle. One day, when we wake up with none of our old towers to ego standing, we'll have to be ready. It would be best to begin to learn about the lost art before desperation to hang onto the old ways sets in, because afterwards learning won't come very easily.

That's the negative line of thinking. On the positive side, let's just try to fondly imagine a time when love and harmony was the rule. We ventured away from home, had adventures and learned a lot. However, now it's time to reconnect to the lines of love that have always surrounded us.

These lifelines have been thrown out to us by our loved ones—our present family members, our ancestors and spiritual guides. Recognition of this love and connection is the first step to remembering the lost art. Learning how to apply it to life's challenges is the next step, and the trick to making this magic work is to remember to translate injury and pain into the perception of opportunity.

For instance, I've had an injured neck most of my life. As I've gotten older the pain has gotten more acute. When I used to move wrong and trigger a spasm, there'd be a knee-jerk reaction to the pain. Yet, just as in all aspects of our lives, learning to send painful body parts that transformational, loving energy is an art, which takes faithful practice.

Eastern philosophy has always had more of an appreciation for the subtleties of healing (and living for that matter), than we do normally here in the West. In his book, *Awaken Healing Energy Through the Tao,* Mantak Chia describes a technique he calls "The Secret of the Inner Smile." He breaks down the concept of sending love to body parts into a science.

Sending a smile and love to something that causes pain will feel innately wrong to most people. Yet if we always do what feels natural, we'll never exercise our Free Will enough to make positive, alchemical changes in our lives. The magic only results when we disengage from our karmicly imposed harmony and tune into a consciously selected one.

During a channeling session with my better half, I was informed that my wife and I were both physicians back in ancient Greece. Back then, that occupation was a multi-disciplinary attempt to reconnect people with a higher harmony. We began by discussing attitudes and potential. Then we used hypnosis in an attempt to get under their limited ego programming.

I was told that I also performed psychic surgery. This is where the practitioner appears to reach into the body and pull out the offending mass so people can better accept their new harmony with health. It's a combination art which uses the One Thing to heal the patient, and then actually manifests a bloody mass (which the patient believes physically came out of their body) to help convince the patient's mind that they are in fact healed. Next to the One Thing, illusion is the most powerful force in the physical world. Psychic surgeons use it to their advantage right along with holistic and harmonic techniques to transform disease into ease.

The first homeopathic remedy resulted from a demonstration of alchemy using a diluted poison infused with loving attention (the sorcerer's stone). The result was the cure to the poison with which they started.

This is a procedure that was found to work so well, that it endured longer than the knowledge of the one essential ingredient. When homeopathic remedies are prepared with more of that loving attention, their alchemical cures are much more dramatic. Still, natural laws are called into action even without it, and so mankind gets by another day in another way without any awareness of the one essential thing.

Still, love and harmony is the nutritious growth goo in the Petri dish of life. Getting intimately familiar with them is the first step to healing what ever needs healing and growing into the loving space we all want.

Sending loving energy to ALL the concerns and people in our lives, will feel real strange at first. Still, love is the one thing, which has power to bring us into harmony with an improved environment. Oneness with our environment is our natural condition even when present conditions put up barriers to our affinity for that nature. We can fight it, as most of us have done for eons. Yet, when we're really ready to make a permanent change we need to learn to do it from the inside out. It's up to us to plant the seed of harmony deep in the heart of what we want to change.

Disappointment in ourselves and in others will always compete for our attention, but we have to gradually give up that addiction.

Our desires and preferences are the fuel, which powers our vehicles down the road of life. Personal choices create our momentum. However, harmony with our higher selves is what steers us in constructive directions. Expecting harmony and being open to inner guidance can transform any bad trip into a magical one. When we do this we're still using our preferences and power, but instead of forcing our way, we learn to bravely stand our ground waiting for the *One Thing* to work its magic.

Seeing the reality of this ride, we learn to slow down, control our reactions, and *act more maturely*. We learn to keep our vehicles between the ditches. However, *actually BEING mature* is a matter of taking the responsibility for maneuvering our vehicles down that road to the absolute best of our ability.

This entails coming into harmony with everything around us. It's all about watching way ahead of where we are, anticipating curves, and watching all the signs carefully. It entails taking care of our own life, anyone traveling with us, and anyone who comes into our path. Ultimately, it's the art of knowing our vehicle and becoming one with the road.

As mature souls, we grow into an intimate knowledge of the influences that govern our existence and learn to co-create with them. We get to know and love our own nature and the nature of all things. We learn to hug the road wherever it takes us!

Mastery of the mystic art of alchemy comes when we learn to confidently extend our love into all the friendly AND unfriendly influences in our lives. Open hearted communication with all our friends and enemies, family and spiritual guides, leads to an increasing appreciation for them and a better harmony with their influence. Gradually, love grows into areas that we used to hold at a distance because of our preconceived priorities for our own way.

When love grows into those areas, harmony feeds a conscious cooperation with what we used to think was just background noise. That's when the almost imperceptible noise of our inner nudges becomes clearer. It's also what causes the "in your face" noise of unwanted social relations to either vanish or transform into something very different.

I've often had trouble with long-term social relations. However, like the pain in my neck, they present an opportunity to try my hand at alchemy. The lost art isn't lost. It's just been forgotten, and together we can bring it back.

The first step is to recognize the tremendous amount of the *one* essential *thing* all around us. Focus on it. Let your actions, words and silence sprout from it. Dedicate yourself solemnly to its sacredness and/ or sprinkle it playfully like fairy dust wherever you go. When you can see that your own preferences are only part of the mind of this essential *thing*, no matter how you work with it, the result is bound to be magical! Then, as you get to know your union with it, even the most leaded life is bound to turn into gold!

8

Harmonizing with Nature

The source of thy Spirit is drawn from Earth's heart, for in thy form thou art one with the Earth.
—The Emerald Tablets of Thoth

Nature is our friend. The idea that we need to overpower Mother Nature or overcome our own personal nature is what has caused most of our problems over the centuries. However good or bad it may seem, there is only One Nature. Or as William Shakespeare once put it: "There is nothing good or bad but thinking makes it so."

I discussed the *One Thing* in the previous two chapters in an attempt to convey the nature of God and the nature of "good." Knowing that there is no other essential thing besides this *One Thing*, helps us harmonize with it.

For instance, I lived a particularly nasty past life as an evil magician who helped Genghis Kahn dispose of his enemies. When that life was over, there weren't any black, smoky beings that pulled me off to purgatory like there always are in movies. There was no angry judge to condemn me. If I had broken off relations with my higher self, it would probably have gone differently. As it was, I met with my higher self as I always did between lives. Together we worked with others and planned my next life.

I'm not saying that no one can ever come into harmony with Hell, and duality certainly exists in the dualistic worlds. However, our true home is by nature outside the dualistic world. There can be carry-over into the afterlife if that's what we expect, and lessons usually continue, because that's in our best interest.

People who plan on going to Hell or purgatory probably will spend some time there, but it'll be of their own creation. Then, if they don't find a way out or get rescued, they'll die there, and it'll be back to business as usual in the physical world after a quick respite to regroup and plan their next physical life.

Nothing is forever except the One Nature of the One God. Focusing on that One Nature helps us avoid experiencing anything else of a contrary nature that we may otherwise create. Even an evil, murderous magician has the same essential nature as a priest, a student of Socrates and Pythagoras, or, for instance, as someone who has maybe broken a contract with death by coming into harmony with a higher purpose. I know that all for a fact!

> *Darkness and Light are both of the one nature, different only in seeming, for each arose from the source of all. Darkness transmuted is light of the Light. This, my children, is your purpose in being; transmutation of darkness to Light.*
> *– The Emerald Tablets of Thoth.*

There aren't two kinds of people any more than there are two kinds of nature. Nature within and without is all good. As a society, we've become distracted and deceived. However, where there is disease, ease can be introduced through harmony with our one essential nature.

Social norms are going through a lot of changes right now, and that will only speed up and intensify until at least 2012. To some degree we are all connected with the mass human consciousness. I can tell you from experience that the answer isn't to try to disconnect from this consciousness or society, and we certainly can't personally take on all the "bad guys."

The only real answer is found in that *thing* which is more common than dirt but more misunderstood than any thing else. When we hold onto the knowledge of our unity with this all-pervading love, our uniqueness as individuals and our unity with society all falls right into place.

Mother Nature is also going to be manifesting some big changes in the near future. Not to be an alarmist, but there is going to be some serious death and destruction through 2014 or so. Still, the point here is that manifestations of change don't affect the essence of a thing any more than waves on the surface of the water effect the composition of the ocean. It's human nature to look for depth and clarity with the expectation that what we'll find down deep will look the same as things do on the surface.

For instance, we tend to think that if things are really good, they should always look good with everyone happy, healthy and safe. A good development that involves death of the physical body for instance, is usually beyond the comfort level of most people. The idea of dispelling the illusion of duality, as grand as that possibility may be, will be seen as totally irrelevant to most people if it involves any discomfort or necessitates a change of plans.

Our Earth is a three dimensional entity (which is rapidly evolving into the fifth dimension.) When we imagine all the depth below the surface, we can see that expecting things at her core to be similar to the grass and trees on her surface is a little unrealistic. "To err is human." To err over and over and over is human. However, eventually coming to know what is right in front of us is within human nature too.

We tend to fear what we don't understand, and we can't see what is going on beneath the surface of things. However, we can come to know its nature. Judging the heart of Mother Earth by the cracks in her skin or wind in her hair is going to be increasingly deceiving. Similarly, reacting with fear to the manifestations of the *One Thing* is to give up our power to the winds of illusion. Nothing can move those who stand firm with a tight grip on the Sorcerer's Stone.

The *One Thing* at the heart of Mother Nature is only evolving to a higher degree of expression. One of the manifestations of change she must undergo in this process for herself and for us is the lowering of her magnetism and a shifting of her magnetic fields. This has been happening in small phases, and it will continue to happen slowly but in increasing degrees, probably right up until 2013 to 2014. At that point, Billy confirmed that the magnetic north will have shifted about 160 degrees from where it was recorded in the 1990s, before the magnetic lines started moving much.

NASA just discovered in December of 2008 that there's a breach in the Earth's magnetic field that is ten times larger than any gap they've previously discovered. The sun has been channeling higher dimension energy though this gap to fortify the Earth's energy grid, which is just one initial step that helps the Earth make the transformation to the higher dimension. Another step, which has been prophesized by many for quite a while, is a magnetic pole shift.

The Emerald Tablets of Thoth states that every time we get half way around the precession of the equinox, the poles shift to some degree as a result of the Earth's magnetism dropping. This is part of the natural order that occurs twice in her 25,920 year-long trip around the procession of the equinox. We all exercise our Free Will for about 13,000 years, until the earth reaches a certain point midway around the equinox. Then, for a short while, our mother exercises hers before we continue on our way for another 13,000 years, completing the cycle.

In their September 9, 2004, article entitled, "Earth's Magnetic Field is Fading," *National Geographic News* reported that since 1845, the Earth's magnetism has weakened 10%. In *Beyond Prophecies and Predictions,* Moira Timms says, "During the past 1,800 years, this (magnetic) field is estimated to have fallen to less than two-thirds of its original strength."

Professor Bannerjee, of the University of New Mexico, has stated that Earth's magnetism has dropped 50% in the last 4,000 years. Vince Migliore, editor of the *Geo-Monitor Newsletter,* says that on a magnetic scale of 1–10, our magnetic field is at about 1.5.

Whatever, the exact decline of magnetism, the point is that it's definitely declining. Besides the understandable interruption in your cell phone and satellite reception, there is another little wrinkle in the magnetic drop process. The "as above so below" principle applies again here.

The magnetic field around the Earth feeds the magnetic fields around our brains and within each individual brain cell. Our memory and synaptic functions are dependent on this magnetic field remaining strong. When the field drops, things don't work right.

The early Russian space program discovered that when people go out into space away from the magnetism of the Earth for more than two weeks, they literally go crazy. Their scientists created a little device to be worn on their belts which creates a magnetic field so this won't happen. However, providing everyone in the world with one of these to compensate for the dropping magnetism isn't high on the priorities of our rulers.

Billy confirmed what we all know—people have been getting crazier all the time. This is mainly due to the drop in magnetism. He also said that right before the big shifts, when magnetism seriously drops, people will seriously loose it if they're inclined to. However, as our logical brains lose functionality, our hearts can become more functional and harmony with nature becomes easier.

This is the way Mother Earth periodically fine-tunes humanity. She usually drops her magnetism gradually, and this time will be one of the most gradual. This helps mankind come back into harmony with the Earth in a slow and natural way, especially if we cooperate with the process. Yet, regardless of how abrupt this lowering of magnetism is, it always facilitates a much-needed reunion with Mother Earth every 13,000 years.

Gregg Braden explains why the dropping magnetism affects us this way: "Dense magnetics lock in emotional and mental patterns from generation to generation in the morphogenetic field. With lesser magnetic fields, this seems to ease up, allowing easier access to higher states, as the cells of our body tune to, and try to match, Earth's frequency…"

This is a natural function of our body. We don't really have to consciously do anything. However, we can fight it. We can go a little crazy. That's a natural reaction too. It's our choice, but harmonizing is better. In other words, now would be a good time to dust off that old art of alchemy so we can mitigate the damage of events which go contrary to our plans.

It's said that parts of the Egyptian pyramids are constructed so that they somehow have less magnetism than anywhere else. They were constructed this way to help initiates let go of their "emotional and mental patterns" so they could come into better harmony with nature.

We are so fortunate to be living in a time when we don't have to travel to Egypt or climb into a dirty old pyramid just to enjoy the benefits of lower magnetism! With Mother Earth's help, we can let go our emotional mindsets right now. And this blessing is only going to be increasing up until the time of the shift.

At the end of the Atlantean period, Mother Nature dropped her magnetism suddenly to near zero for a while in order to totally reboot the human civilization. Most of mankind's memories were lost, and manmade materials vanished. People reverted to a primal mode of operation, and it took about 5,000 years for them to get their bearings and get start to make progress again. This has happened before too, but it doesn't usually happen. Every half way around the procession of the equinox, Mother Earth has several options open to her.

Magnetism always drops as a retuning measure, but how much it drops depends on how much retuning is necessary. The Earth will wobble a little. The magnetic poles will drift some, but a big, sudden change in magnetism is always optional. When you consider that magnetism drops some every 13,000 years, dropping a lot, as indicated by complete reversals in the magnetic flow patterns is relatively rare. According to Braden, in the last 76 million years, only 171 reversals have been recorded.

If her people are ready for a dimensional shift, this is when it can happen. Since mankind first appeared on Earth, all of these dimensional shifts except one have been downward. This was to match the lowering of the Earth's frequency which was in response to the increased desire for contrast among mankind. The one upward shift happened at the beginning of the Atlantean period. Then, the people brought on a serious downward shift in consciousness at the end of the Atlantean period which was precipitated and accentuated by an experiment that got out of control.

Preceding all of these shifts, and coinciding with sudden magnetic slippage, there has always been a void of about 30 hours to 3½ days. The void between the dimensions helps us keep the coloring of our experiences between the lines. Magnetics has always had to drop to the point where we lose physical consciousness, so we could experience the new unity conscious perspective and bring it back with us to help renew our world.

Or, if we were changing dimensions as a group at those times, it made for a clean break, like restarting your computer with a new program.

This drop in magnetism to near zero sends people into the void by releasing them from all mental and emotional ties to what they have known up to that point. This drop in magnetism and resulting drop in emotional and mental baggage helps us get in touch with our underlying nature. During the time in the black void, people experience a profound oneness with all nature. They aren't aware of anything else except this oneness. So when they emerge into a new reality, shock is minimized, and they're better prepared to start off in harmony with whatever they find in that new world.

If magnetics drop to near zero long enough, normal people lose their memories. If magnetics stay at or near zero even longer, all synthetic manmade materials lose their cohesiveness, fall apart and disappear. That's why the ancient builders used 25 ton natural rock blocks to build the pyramids and up to 200-ton blocks other places (which, by the way, are totally impossible to build today even with our modern technology) instead of light-weight, easy to handle, high-tech alloy building materials. If you want to be sure that what you build will last through the next shift, you use the durable materials which have always been around.

I'll tell you what to expect for the coming shift later, but there won't be a prolonged void if one happens at all. When the dimensional shift happens, about a year or so after the magnetic and physical shifting of the earth (and a possible short void), those who are ready will just consciously move into the next dimension. Also, magnetism won't drop to near zero for very long, so we won't lose our memories. However, maintaining complete sanity is already beginning to become a challenge. That's why, "Now's the time to find your center."

Those were Billy's words. My translation would be, "Now's the time to come into harmony with your heart and nature." Now's the time to practice faith in the *One Thing*, so no matter what we lose on the mental level, we'll still be in tight with what's real. Picture someone holding onto the stone of harmony as a hurricane swirls around them. The heart has a mind all of its own—literally! Also, finding our center, clinging to the

One real Thing, creates a balanced energy all its own, and could actually keep mind and life in tact.

Edgar Casey once said, "Many a land could be kept intact by the consciousness of its inhabitants."

Hopi prophesy predicts that the land under those faithful to the ways of Mother Earth will, "raise like plateaus" above all the chaos.

What they say sounds like either fantasy or magic. That's because they're referring to an art which is, for all intents and purposes, lost to the world. The science of alchemy has been relegated to the status of a myth. Yet, if ever there's a time to get to the bottom of that myth, this would be it!

When I asked how our home would hold up to the coming big winds, I was told we'd be fine because the house is "well-grounded." By this he meant that we had sanctified the home and area, and Mother Nature recognized it as part of herself. I asked about our guesthouse, and he said it's "grounded enough." When I asked about a house next door where I know the people are very disconnected, he smiled and said that it's not grounded at all, and that's why most of it will probably be blown down.

These predictions are based on the natural, alchemical Man-Earth connection that is still not understood by science. Things which demonstrate this connection only look like miracles because we don't understand them. Regardless of what happens on the physical level, learning the care and feeding of the human spirit is what's really important. When that base is covered, all related physical manifestations eventually fall into place.

Ignorance of our connection with Nature can take many forms. In past eras, people used to think that when things went bad, God was punishing them for something they did wrong. Today, most people think there's no intelligence behind catastrophic "acts of God." Why is it so hard to understand that being out of harmony with Nature could have adverse consequences? When we breathe in an allergen, the natural reaction is to try to sneeze it out. When dog has fleas, it tries to scratch them off. The

Earth is sneezing and scratching at its disharmonious parts. You don't have to be a dumper of toxic waste to get her attention either.

Mother Earth is no more merely rock and water than we are simply flesh and blood. She's an enlightened soul that constantly scans the surface of her body, our planet, for activity, attitude and intent. She may seem to paint new pictures with broad brush stroke sometimes. However, a harmonious relationship with our inner guidance along with a harmonious relationship with Nature will assure that we're always where we need to be.

When I picture faith in this connection and courage in the face of the cyclone of destruction, I imagine the most spiritual person I know, Drunvalo Melchizedek, sitting in a teepee with the flap open smiling as Nature blows debris and destruction all around him. I can see him closing the flap, and his little teepee hugging the ground as hurricane force winds blow all around him. Maybe he'll have a loved one or two in his little teepee who'll have the blessing of seeing his total faith up close and personal. This isn't a prediction. It's just the personal image I hold in my heart and head to remind me of what a good connection and faith in the Universe looks like.

> A human being is part of the whole, called by us
> 'universe'… He experiences himself, his thoughts and
> feelings as something separated from the rest—a
> kind of optical delusion of his consciousness… Our
> task must be to free ourselves from our prison by
> widening our circle of compassion to embrace all
> humanity and the whole of Nature in its beauty.
> – Albert Einstein

Practice harmonizing with nature and the presence of the *One Thing*, and you'll react right when the time comes. In the meantime, don't worry about the drop in magnetism, or the cyclone of world events, or the possible whirlwind of disappointing personal experiences around you. Look for the beauty and order of nature. Know that it's there, no matter how hidden it is, and that everything is proceeding according to plan. When you can see God in all people and situations without judging or second guessing his/her/its purpose, you're ready to weather all the changes nicely in the peaceful eye of the storm.

I was accused of being "aloof" today. So, I thought I should include a peek into my life and personal thoughts just to show everyone that I'm not talking out of an "ivory tower."

9

A Live Experiment

Preface

This journal lays out what I see happening in my own life, complete with my personal anguish, doubts and realizations, as I wrote the rest of the book from that last chapter on. If I was a reader, I think I'd like to see the personal tests and insights I underwent while writing this book. However, not to get too bogged down, I put most of it in as an appendix.

JUNE 27, 2007, THE GUINEA PIG SPEAKS: I was accused of being "aloof" today. So, I thought I should include a peek into my life and personal thoughts just to show everyone that I'm not talking out of an "ivory tower." I have many stories that I could have included in the first couple of chapters to illustrate my utter mortality. However, I decided to just touch on a few so I could maintain an upbeat mood and a clearly positive philosophy in my writing.

This journal should give that positive philosophy depth by showing my human struggle between faith and the challenges of reality. I've painstakingly researched the workings of life, and my life in particular, on every level I can in an attempt to see what's actually going on. The more we see, the easier it is to have faith. Still, knowing something is true and really internalizing it so you prove it in your own life are two different things.

I know some people lead charmed lives. Also, some academic types are really insulated from the real world. Sometimes I have regrets about not taking that path, but now it's my good fortune to be able to write from a point of view well balanced in the life issues, which beset all normal people. So, for the sake of realism I'm going to share what's going on in my life, what I think about it, and keep writing this journal until I have a happy ending.

See the appendix for more.

10

The New Energetic Template

Life is a series of natural and spontaneous changes. Don't resist them—that only creates sorrow. Let reality be reality. Let things flow naturally forward in whatever way they like.
—Lao-Tzu

The epitome of wisdom has always been to try not to become stuck in our ideas of who we are or what we want. We're told we need to accept life for what it is, listen to Spirit and tune into who we really are, so we can come to understand what we're really supposed to do in this life. Behind this sage advice is the fact that before we entered this life we consciously worked with our higher self and every significant person in our life today to create a contract.

These contracts invariably include conflict as a motivation for learning the lessons our higher self wants to firmly embed into our awareness. So problems aren't necessarily a sign that we're doing anything wrong. As humans, it's nearly impossible to see the divine purpose behind the conflicts in front of us, or the divinity in those with whom we have conflicts.

For that reason, the spiritual message has always been to try to stay flexible, go with the flow, and to listen to the inner guides who will lead you back to "the path." This path, of course, is the life contract we helped plan back on the other side when we could see clearly, before we arrived in this world.

The message of trying to come into harmony with this divinely ordained path, which is imbedded in our nature (as defined by our DNA and the life situations we chose before entering this world), is the primary spiritual advice given on any other dualistic world, and what Lao-Tzu said about going with the flow is generally really good advice here too.

The difference with those of us on Earth is that our nature is challenged and aggravated by Free Will. Free Will is really a divine quality, which the human mind generally hasn't been able to incorporate into our human nature. So, our reactions to it have been erratic, and we've generally abused that gift throughout the ages. We've misunderstood it and taken it for granted as much as we have the *One Thing*.

Now, with the new Earth grid in place, the *One Thing* is being rediscovered. We're growing into a mature understanding of it and of its beloved offspring, Free Will. Between now and the shift, those who evolve with the Earth to the next dimension WILL learn to use Free Will properly. That is what will enable us to abandon our 3-D contracts and our old nature in favor of a better way.

It's hard to believe things can change so quickly. Historically, one person's dream of Free Will has generally been realized by imposing a nightmare on another's. This can be seen in the acts of conquerors throughout the ages like Genghis Khan, Julius Caesar, Alexander "The Great," Napoleon, Adolph Hitler, Christopher Columbus, and one or two modern national leaders. Beginning in 200 AD, the church formed a union with the state to help build their mutual empire. This craziness peaked around the time of Don Quixote and the Inquisitions, but has only recently lost its firm hold on the masses.

Still, in the twenty-first century, control of the people has been transferred from the Church and State to worldwide corporations and the State—and the State's actual power may be mostly for show. New inquisitions are staged over issues of patriotism. The Church used to send missionaries and soldiers who would return with a boatload of gold from their conquests. Modern empires like the US now export the new economic religion disguised as democracy to keep their pipelines of black gold flowing and to balance supply and demand issues. The murder and mayhem necessary to achieve their goals isn't any more of a deterrent for our modern conquerors than it was during the dark ages.

The standard presumption has always been that the conqueror's goals are more important than any existing order, which stands in his way of achieving those goals. It's certainly more important than truthful presentation of his real goals to those enlisted to do his bidding. The conqueror's goals are sold to the masses with justifications like loyalty, nationality, and religious righteousness; "our way of life," "Mom and apple pie…"

As Mark Twain put it, "Those who don't read the newspapers are uninformed. Those who do read the newspapers are misinformed."

We are just now beginning to see the motives of the world conquerors for what they are. It wasn't that long ago that we called the ones in control "gods." These were the guys who stripped our inner knowing away with their self-serving genetic manipulations (we'll get to that in the next chapter).

After these "gods" left, our kings, who were supposedly messengers of the gods, continued to impose absolute authority and control over our assets and lives. When we began to make spiritual headway, despite the genetic limitations imposed on us, as we did many times throughout history, such as during the Golden Age of Greece, these rulers ruthlessly disregarded and destroyed that progress and our Free Will, in order to stake their claim and enforce their tribute. The machine of their empire would run on by running all over the Free Will of others.

For Free Will to work as intended, we need to work with our higher selves as we did when making our life contracts before entering this world. However, that's nearly impossible while we're working with human perception (which was forcibly reduced) in the heaviness of 3-D realities. We know what we want, and that's usually as far as our consciousness goes. Yet, the consequences of surrendering to that limitation are all too clear from a quick scan of history or even the daily news.

This should be inspiration enough for all of us to clean up our personal priorities. When we hold a generous, well meaning intent, our higher selves can take care of the particular arrangements to assure that the good of the whole isn't overlooked. This leaves us free to lead our lives knowing that our Free Will is integrating into the Free Will of others, bringing about the highest good for all involved in our situations and relationships.

Observing the misuse of power around us is the first step to learning to take personal responsibility for the proper handling of our own Free Will. The big world is sadly a reflection of our little ones. However, individual lives can change, and when our priorities and goals change, the whole world changes.

News flash: the whole world is changing. Changing priorities are causing the world to respond—which, in turn, is opening up new opportunities for us. Going with the flow is no longer always the best possible option. As Adam R. Gwizdala put it, "If you go with the flow you'll eventually end up over the waterfall."

> In a live Kryon channeling by Lee Carroll in September and October 2005 called Un-defining The Spiritual Path, Kryon says: "We told you it's like purchasing a ticket on a spiritual train, which you call your path, and then being patient until the train gets there. Well, it's graduation time. We're going to change that metaphor to something far more complex. If you want to purchase the ticket, that's fine. That's called intent. But there is no track, and there is no train! Oh, but there's a station! What are you going to do at the station when there's no train and no track? You're going to be laughed at. Well, the track and train are not built yet. "Who's going to build them?" "You are."
> – Lee Carroll, The Kryon Writings

For almost all people, there's always a train coming along on a pre-agreed schedule and going to a divinely ordained destination. The basic wisdom of the dualistic world is to be patient and wait for the right train. Be comfortable with the knowledge that there is a divine plan at work and that you're part of it.

However, as Kryon pointed out, now we're looking at another possibility. We no longer have to be satisfied with old priorities and goals based on uncomfortable realities. There's suddenly a new possibility in front of us which allows us to make some serious personal changes, which translate into some serious social changes.

This new possibility has been provided for by the recent accomplishment of two universal mile stones. Suddenly, our ability to make more and better use of our Free Will has been given a real boost! Now, **reality on all levels is actually changing because of two events.**

First of all, there was a global awakening and coming into harmony with the *One Thing* which culminated on August 16th, and 17th in 1987. This has been called the harmonic convergence. As a planet, a degree of enlightenment hit critical mass, and we took a major step toward converging on a harmony with the One Nature of all things.

Then, in 1989, the new grid of enlightened consciousness around the world was completed. Actually, Billy informed me that it has been *recreated* after being reduced to its former dodecahedronal form during the fall of man just prior to the sinking of Atlantis. In other words, our new grid isn't actually new at all. It's the original structure, which is the template for an order that we lost over 13,000 years ago.

In January, 2008, a ceremony was performed that helped balance the male and female energy of the planet. This made the "new" grid a little more accessible to the masses. So, in essence, it was turned on for many people.

Some call it the "Christ consciousness grid." However, this may be a bit misleading. The purpose of this grid was never to teach us to walk on water. It may carry some cool perks, but it's basically to reinforce our efforts to be humane to each other by reminding us our interconnectedness.

The knowledge of the energy grid and our relationship to it is ancient. Humans have their own grid around them just as all animals do. As long as there are two of any species, they'll also have an energy grid around the whole world, which corresponds to the grid around each beastie of a particular species.

There have always been more than two unity conscious humans on the earth at one time. Yet, they were still humans, and the overpowering number of egocentric conscious humans collapsed our unity consciousness grid. The consensus of consciousness dictates the grid's shape, and so far we've all been compatible enough to be considered one species.

Pythagoras secretly taught his initiates about the sacred dodecahedron around the Universe which was replicated around the Earth, and all of creation. This subject was taught in such a sacred way, that to bring it up, no matter how carefully, outside the school was strictly prohibited on penalty of death. This provision kept the teachings pure and kept the knowledge of the energetic grid in perspective of the whole of Pythagoras's teachings.

Two hundred years later, the sacred subject of the energy grid leaked out and found its way to Plato, where it lost its subtly, sacredness and universal ramifications. Homogenizing the subject for mass consumption, Plato simply blurted out that there was a dodecahedron of energy around the Earth.

One of the significances, which was lost until recently, is the awareness that this energy is holographic of all life, right down to our DNA. Besides the dodecahedron of energy around the Universe and around the Earth, there is one about 52 to 55 feet around every human. This grid also translates down to every living tissue and element here on Earth.

Remember that Egyptian description of the "as above so below" description of *The One Thing?* This grid (above) provides an energetic template for each of the 108 basic elements in our periodic table (below) which interface back with the energy field of the whole planet.

As Yoda, from *Star Wars* put it, "The Force both obeys and commands."

This energy grid around the Earth and everything in it thus maintains order as we know it. However a lot of that order is suddenly changing. With the help of the ascended masters, our grid has evolved. The dodecahedron that Pythagoras and Plato described has changed. It's grown in depth and structure to match the more evolved form that existed before the fall of man.

Getting kicked out of Eden was significant, but it wasn't a "fall," or failure in any regard. However, about 13,500 years ago we had a significant fall in consciousness (which I'll describe later). Then, a little over 1000 years later, after the Great Flood, humanity started over, symbolized by Abraham producing twelve sons.

These twelve sons started twelve tribes, which moved through the twelve constellations of the zodiac. What they learned was fed into the twelve energetic pentagons around the Earth which has caused our planetary dodecahedronal grid to evolve. This foundation has been building, and with the help of the ascended masters, those twelve pentagons on the surface of the dodecahedron now have twelve icosahedral caps, which are five-faced pyramids.

This grid now looks like a three-dimensional star that has twelve points. The loving nature of the energy has never changed. However, this reconstructed structure is much sturdier than our previous one. If you were to actually create these two forms out of cardboard for instance, you'd find that the regular dodecahedron can be collapsed with very little pressure. However, the stellated (star shaped) dodecahedron can't be collapsed nearly as easily.

This new shape isn't just a new and improved package for the nature of all things. It isn't just a convenient comparison to how our love-based priorities are supported by a firmer consciousness. It's actually the foundation of that solid love-based consciousness!

This new Earth grid is the long awaited energetic template which fortifies the nature of the *One Thing* (love) with depth and strength. It is the shape of the rebirth of love on Earth. Down here on Earth, this new love template is translating into more mindfulness of our actions, and an appreciation for the fruits of harmony and peace.

This new shape also gives the *One Thing* a point. Actually it gives it twelve points, each of which defines the one Big Point of love and harmony in different ways. If human love for life were to take a shape, (which it has to in the course of creation) it would take twelve pentagrams and form a dodecahedron. If our divine human nature were to make this love complete, (which it has) it would put five sided, pointed caps on each of these pentagrams to form the stellated dodecahedron.

This is the shape of the energetic grid around the earth which is now empowering the loving nature of the *One Thing* and harmonizing our evolution with its intent. Picture it glowing with love. My better half says she sees the grid around the earth throwing off white and green sparks. Even its image feels powerful for those who want to harmonize with it and lethal to those who harbor goals of overpowering it.

This new template has been met with great enthusiasm from our space brothers on many dimensions. Their loving support beams down, first reinforcing our new grid and then filtering into our world, filling it with sparkling light and love for all life here. The world is increasingly vibrant with this love. That is the main difference in how our new world will look compared to our old one. I'm supposed to say that so everyone who's planning on coming along for the ride can practice seeing it that way and thus contribute to its stability and power.

Every bit of love we send out to anyone helps light up the grid a little more. The more it's lit, the more it inspires support from the outside. The machine of life is fueled by the same *one thing* it generates. Learning to work more consciously, intimately and harmoniously with this magical *One Thing* powers our evolution forward and is THE purpose of life—in case anyone wondered."

We send love out. It hits the grid stimulating more outside support which results in more love and light and blessings for all of us all the time. Even our cells and DNA are changing. Since we're more in harmony with the One Nature of all things, matter is becoming more responsive to our will. Also, our Free Will is finally beginning to come into harmony with its divine potential.

In other words, we finally have a much better chance of making proper use of Free Will. If we don't like the way things are going, we can put a new intent out into the universe and let our higher self pull things into a more currently-appealing order. Since the change in the Earth Grid, priorities have been shifting, and Free Will can bring us into harmony with this new order quicker than ever before.

The train I had prearranged to ride on was scheduled to take me back to that big roundhouse in the sky. However, the New Earth Grid has changed the order of things down here, and like others, I'm responding to that. My priorities have changed, and I suddenly I have the power to find a new train.

As Kryon explains, now we've graduated. Now our love has depth and an enduring strength. As a race, we're also now coming into the knowledge of our interdependence on others and how to use our Free Will more wisely.

We're throwing out the old instruction manual, and the obvious question would be, "When are we going to get a new one?"

I think it's interesting that the Jehovah's Witnesses have been told that a new bible will be given to them when the new age arrives. I suppose someone could write something that would cover most of the contingencies for a newly enlightened age. However, a definitive work worthy of being called a bible, which answered enough questions to the satisfaction of the modern reader without demanding blind faith to its inconsistencies, would be an extremely complicated process on many levels.

Even if that were possible, once someone wanted personal answers, which is really the purpose of spirituality (as opposed to religion) the written word would be worthless except as a divination technique. A manual could be used to help point the way to your own personal guidance. However, that sort of takes some of the exclusivity out of "God's written word." At any rate, the point is the only true gospel is a personal one. If the Jehovah Witnesses in the new world are going to get a new bible, they're probably each going to have to write their own like everyone else.

Even if a general enlightenment manual could be composed, it would be quickly even more corrupted than the old one has become by attempts to simplify it. Deciphering the proper use of your Free Will has to be a matter between each of us and our higher self. On an encouraging note though, the energetic grid of the entire world is now supporting our highest use of this new possibility.

We used to have gurus who showed us the way. At some point, which varied from individual to individual, we grew up so that we could decipher for ourselves what we were really supposed to do, i.e., how to tune into our own divinely contracted life. Now, many of us are growing into the next option: We're building our own train and track, and setting our own course.

Although I can't tell you how to do that exactly, I can tell you what to expect. Once you let that train go by for which you bought a ticket, the knowledge of what to do next doesn't automatically hit you. Kryon presents a romantic image of free souls happily creating their own trains and tracks in order to not scare us away from taking this very important next evolutionary step. He provides the valuable service of inspiring us to trust our divine abilities and reach for our ultimate potential.

I just thought I'd introduce a little reality into that picture and give you a small idea of what it feels like to be sitting at the station when the train on which you've already booked passage leaves. After eons of conditioning and trying to do what we agreed to in our lifetime, it feels instinctively really wrong to miss that train! As developing beings, we're becoming more conscious of our path and agreements, so that train doesn't usually leave anymore without our knowing it. In my case, when I married before the train with my contracted love had arrived, I simply missed the clues that said "wait for the right train."

Looking back at it, I really believe that my higher self was working with my impatience and lack of faith and anything else he could, to get me to miss that train. As it turned out, that alternative life led to fulfilling my departure from this earth on schedule, according to my pre-life contract. Not a bad thing. In fact, it was a much more satisfying life than the one I actually led, up to my departure point. In my actual life, events leading to that departure date didn't send me all the way back to the other side, but they still delivered a serious shock to my system. Life felt like a losing battle for a couple of decades! Then suddenly, the battle was over, and a new order developed.

I believe this is the way Spirit is transitioning us into this new freedom. Very few, if any, can work with Spirit in the way we did on the other side of the veil, before we came to the physical. We simply don't have the clarity or detachment. However, staying in touch with our higher selves can be a life-saver!

Clarity and detachment grows with our trust in the abilities of our higher selves. So as this trust grows, we grow into harmony with our new powers and potential. The goal that we are approaching is to be able to remake our life contracts with full higher consciousness, so that we can enter into agreements with others, with awareness of that agreement, before we physically meet them.

The goal is to miss the train carrying our old preferences and priorities, and quickly arrange for a new one with all the divine clarity with which we planned our original itinerary while we were on the brighter side of the veil. I expect we'll have a lot more of that clarity after our upcoming ascension. However, for now we have to take our miracles in small doses and keep an open mind about what's possible.

What's possible, in a word, is, "Anything!" Generally, people can do much more with Free Will than they ever could in the past. For instance, people on Earth could always make judgment calls and small detours, which weren't planed for in their contract.

However, until recently, detours or not, everyone generally completed their contract on time. That part of the contract is pretty important, because after your time is up, your life is suddenly in a void until you have a meeting of the minds with your higher self. The ability to consciously do that and the power to change your contract by continuing in this world is just a sign of things to come. Our inherent capability to use Free Will and creativity is unlimited. We may be mere humans, but our immediate potential is now more infinite than ever!

Have you ever wondered how we came to find ourselves in this unique position? It's not just human egotism that tells us that we're special. Yet why were we chosen to be the recipients of divine Free Will when no other dualistic race ever was? The reason for that is a fascinating story, and I don't believe it has ever been told.

In order to make up for what was taken away, and to give her people a chance to eventually regain their sovereignty, she (Mother earth) requested that they be given divine Free Will...NO other dualistic race living on Earth or anywhere else ever had the divine power to make choices, which weren't hard wired into their karmic nature until it was given to the *Homo sapiens*.

11

Man and Mother

...so do all created things come from this One Thing through Transformation.
It's father is the Sun; its mother the Moon.
The Wind carries it in its belly.
Its nurse is the Earth.
                              —Hermes Trismegistus, *The Emerald Tablet*

Mankind was incubated and nursed along by Mother Earth until the winds of change intervened. When her children were stolen, her great love for us initiated a transformation which we're just now beginning to understand. Looking over our known history, we see constant conflict and struggle. However, there's more to our history than meets the eye. Life wasn't always about conflict, and thanks to Mother Earth, there is an end in sight if we can just come into harmony with our Mother and the *One Thing*.

Once, when I asked about ancient history, Billy suggested I read *The 12th Planet* by Zecharia Sitchin. I read just enough to satisfy my own curiosity and fill in the blanks in my understanding so I could write this chapter. However, WHEN you want to know more than my quick summary, Zecharia's book, which is the result of 30 years of research, is well worth looking over.

I've taken Zecharia's findings and have thrown in a couple of my own discoveries, which aren't on any earthly tablets for the translating. The result is a short synopsis of the significance of our history that the average person (like me) can remember. This brevity also made it easier to confirm the essentials through Billy. So, here it is as short and sweet as I can make it:

Our story starts about 450,000 years ago, when a group of ET's called the Nefilim, decided to take up residence on Earth. They were here to mine our raw materials, primarily gold. Incidentally, their industrial need for gold is the root of the value we've placed on that metal throughout history. The Nefilim brought another race of beings with them called the Anunnaki to do all the hard work.

They came during the middle of the Second glacial period, and most of the Earth was fairly inhospitable. However, the Middle East was relatively warm, and it had lots fossil fuels which they used just as we do today. They called the place they landed "Babylon," which in Sumerian means "The Gateway of the gods." I'm afraid the original meaning of "god" has gotten hopelessly confused in the last 400,000 years of propaganda, but suffice to say these guys were not Gods.

After about 150,000 years of working the mines, the Anunnaki began to rebel. Here is a translation of an ancient Sumerian record: "Every single one of us gods has war declared! ...in the excavations; excessive toil has killed us. Our work was heavy, the distress much."

Labor went to management with their list of complaints. "Every day... The lamentation was heavy, we could hear the complaint."

The solution they hit on was to create a lulu. This is often translated as "primitive," but it literally means "one who is mixed." According to the *Free Dictionary* by Fairfax, a lulu is "a remarkable person, object or idea." To begin mixing up their first batch of the remarkable people we call *Homo Sapien*, they called in Mami, who was called the Mother of the gods. I don't know if the ancient Sumerian word lulu is actually the root of the modern word, "lulu" or if Mami is actually the root of our similar sounding word meaning "mother," but those current meanings are a fun way to remember those words.

Mami worked with a geneticist, but ended up taking most of the credit for the creation: "I have completed it... I have removed your heavy work. I have imposed your toil on The Worker, "Man." You raised a cry for a Worker-kind: I have loosed the yoke; I have provided your freedom."

Obviously, they created us to work. The Sumerian term, *"avod,"* usually translated as "worship," actually means to "work." We were custom designed to obey and work for the gods, which is a productive form of "worship" I suppose. Also, after the rebellion of the Anunnaki, the Nefilim were very careful to keep their new workers in their place. This led to fear, and the idea of working in fear led to our understanding of "worship." They had created the legacy of "good, god-fearing men" which somehow still lives on today.

At any rate, the Nefilim worked with *Homo erectus*, who was the result of an earlier seeding of our world by theirs, so the DNA was compatible. They called him their raw material or "mud of the Earth." This project served a couple purposes. First of all, it provided for a necessity: They needed a replacement, less rebellious, worker. They had little respect for these hairy beasts that ate the vegetation and drank water from the ditches like the other animals, which led to their other, more malevolent purpose. The aloof Nefilim were really irritated for a very long time by these beasts who would protect the animals by breaking the hunter's traps and filing in the ditches designed to catch prey.

So, when they began experimenting, they did so with a vengeance. They wanted to make their new man to be more docile and less intelligent. They immediately whacked the 12-strand DNA which *Homo erectus* originally had down to two. This shortened his life span from about 400-500 years (according to Billy) way down so that before their beasts wised up, they'd be dead. The new species was more manageable in other ways too. He didn't have his telepathic abilities anymore, so he couldn't read his creators' true intentions. This also cut him off from clear communication with his own kind, so an organized uprising was much less likely. They fought more among themselves and were much easier to control with simple brute force.

They used Nefilim DNA, thus creating us in their image, and manipulated the genetics until they got the all the qualities they wanted. They made beasts with two heads, ones with four faces, wings, and just about anything else you can imagine. Many of their failures had serious and often fatal physical flaws. However, they eventually got it right.

These child humans were immediately put to work in the gardens (Eden) and in the mines. *Homo erectus* had been on its own evolutionary path when they were hunted down and totally eradicated as a species.

The Nefilim took away their life, and any hope they had for ever regaining control over their own future.

This creation story is disturbing on several levels. One particularly upsetting aspect to it is the total lack of any divine involvement. However, although "God" didn't actually create *Homo sapiens* out of the "mud of the earth," he/she/it was about to get involved.

Because the new species was mixed from two different species, they were infertile just like mules (which are a cross between a horse and a donkey). These human mules were mass-produced and worked naked in the mines and garden like animals. Also, like mules, they basically had no sex drive and were infertile.

Then, the being the Bible calls a serpent comes into the garden. The glyph which was translated as the Sumerian root of the word "serpent" (*nahash*) might very well have been *nhsh* which means "to decipher or to find out." The latter translation would seem to make more sense because this being began more genetic experiments to see what he could find out.

He took pity on this new species, which just had just been totally stripped of any dignity or personal potential. So, he spliced in two sex genes so they could reproduce, and tweaked some other things to enhance desire and pleasure to make procreation more productive. Suddenly, man **and** woman woke up! They saw that they were naked, and discovered the joys of self-indulgent, marathon sex.

They began reproducing like crazy. Their bosses were furious. However, instead of exterminating them (yet), they simply banished them off to the east of Eden. The Nefilim went back to working their human mules, and this new race began to evolve on their own.

This is where this story gets really good. This is the point where divine intervention steps in with a miracle, which had never been granted to any other dualistic race since THE beginning. This is the true story of how our tragic loss of self-determination was transformed to a blessing which made us significantly different than anyone else in the dualistic Universe!

When the Nefilim took away any control the Earth's people had over their own lives, Mother Earth took notice, but sending us love wasn't enough. So, when they gave us the ability to reproduce, Mother Earth sent out a very powerful prayer. Her request was taken all the way to the top, and the White Brotherhood (whose name refers to their light and not skin color) had the privilege of delivering the answer back to her.

Mother Earth had volunteered to house an experiment of her own. In order to make up for what was taken away, and to give her people a chance to eventually regain their sovereignty, she requested that they be given divine Free Will. The Nefilim didn't have divine Free Will. The beings that occupied Lemuria and later Atlantis, as enlightened as their nature was at one time, didn't have Free Will. NO other dualistic race living on Earth or anywhere else ever had the divine power to make choices, which weren't hard-wired into their karmic nature until it was given to the Homo sapiens.

Actually, it was beamed into the Earth grid, which was shared by all humanoids living on the earth. So, all the races that made their home here drew it into their own personal energy grid. Homo sapiens were also compatible sexually with all of them, so one united race quickly developed.

Instantly, decisions became radical. Free Will caused conflict within everyone's nature. We suddenly began to feel things deeper and act in more exaggerated ways. This translated to an immediate escalation in violence. From the time Cain killed Abel, people all over asserted themselves causing chaos which only escalated over the centuries. Finally, after about 20,000 years, mankind is beginning to learn to use this divine Free Will to relate to Spirit with a working understanding of the divine laws. Finally, with just five years before the end of the era, we're beginning to use our Free Will the way it was always hoped we would!

However, back at the beginning, life was going from bad to worse for the new *Homo sapiens*. Now that their sex instincts were ramped up, they drew the attentions of many of the Nefilim and the Anunnaki. The problem is stated in Genesis 6 this way:

> *...the sons of the deities saw the daughters of the Earthlings that they were compatible, and they took unto themselves wives of whichever they chose.*

This made the pure-bred Nefilim angry. Luckily, Enosh and others went back to the Nefilim. Working for them was all they knew. This appeased the gods somewhat who then allowed this group back into their service. The significance here is that a few humans were on the good side of gods when the vote was taken to exterminate them.

It's interesting that the problem was the diluting of the Nefilim bloodline, because the favorites of the gods were the hybrids. Noah, who was 600 years old at the time of the Flood was part "god" (according to Billy), and his grandfather, Methuselah, whose name means "man of the missile," (whether he was born or conceived on the missile) definitely wasn't a purebred Homo sapien. If, as Billy says, humans lived 400 to 500 years before they got their DNA whacked, then anyone who lived more that 400 years after that was definitely part some sort of ET. I think that applies to most of the ten generations between Adam and Noah.

It was a group decision to exterminate the hybrid humans and everyone on earth with them. However, the dynamics were really between two brothers. One was busy manipulating humans to make them easier to control. This brother, who genetically spliced out our psychic abilities and reduced our intelligence and longevity to keep us subservient, was the closest thing mankind had to a "good guy." The other brother thought we would always be too much trouble to bother with. He argued that they should just exterminate all the humans, and his proposal won the vote.

The Atlantean tragedy (explained in the next chapter) brought on earth changes ahead of its natural cycle. So, when the time finally came that the Earth was in the proper position along the procession of the equinox for magnetics to drop and changes to occur, there was no necessity for the Earth to purge humanity any further. The Earth responded by making the necessary adjustments so it could coast through that time with relative peace. When the ancient rulers realized that nothing natural was going to happen, they decided to take things into their own hands.

The plan was to abandon the Earth project for a while, pack up their space ships and blast off huge hunks of the earth's ice caps from a low orbit. This would cause them to fall into the oceans creating thousand foot tidal waves which would swamp the world, so they'd be done with the human experiment once and for all.

Against his brother's wishes, the guy who was dedicated to his project of inventing new and improved slaves leaked the word out to someone who told Noah about the coming flood. Noah was told what to do about it and given the seeds (DNA) of every animal he had categorized for safe keeping on the ark: "Tear down the house, build a ship! Give up possessions, seek tho life! Foreswear belongings, keep soul alive! Aboard ship take thou the seed of all living things. That ship thou shalt build…" Then he gave him exact directions on how to build a teba or "sunken" ship, a submersible ship that proved to be a uniquely seaworthy vessel!

He had seven days to build it, while the gods got all their belongings on their ships and prepared to take off. It's true that many people thought he was crazy. Still, there were many friends, neighbors and craftsmen who all pitched in to help him build it just to be on the safe side. They were all on board when Noah finally stepped on at the last minute.

Everything went according to plan. The Nefilim, many of whom had friends and lovers down on Earth, took off and allowed the plan to proceed. There were tears on board the god's ship as the waves came pouring over the landscape and millions perished. The tidal waves and floods pretty much covered the entire world.

When they landed, the leaders were furious to discover that some humans had survived, but others were relieved. When the flood waters resided, there was probably less than two million people (about half of which were Homo sapiens) left in the world compared to about 64 million before the flood (and the 6.6 billion we have in 2008).

In the five thousand years or so between their creation and the great flood, Homo sapiens had spread pretty much all over the world and multiplied prolifically. They holed up with others during the floods on mountain top communities and in spots that the floods somehow missed. The decision was finally made to leave the job unfinished. The Nefilim vowed to leave humans alone, and left our planet shortly after that. Their planet was moving farther out of reach of Earth and they had to go. Some Nefilim decided to stay on Earth when their people left. This made these slightly higher vibrational beings subject to the same 3-D, dualistic realities as everyone else, but they also inherited Free Will.

❧❧❧

Shortly after the Nefilim left, the reptilian race moved in as if they owned the place. But that's another story. Despite this new, powerful enemy who mated with the Aryans to maintain the appearance of being human, mankind finally had a fighting chance at a new beginning. There were still some heavy handed rulers, but at least we weren't naked mules working for the gods in the garden and mines anymore.

There had been seven root races which made up the Atlantean race. Then, the Atlantean race was one of five races that were homogenized into our world after their fall. One at a time, each race has its day in the sun. It conquers and rules the earth until another race conquers and rules.

According to the tenets of theosophy, there will be two more root races in our time. The sixth race will follow the currently ruling fifth "Aryan race" (which is comprised of seven root races itself). It will be radically more enlightened and personally powerful.

However, what theosophy or any other study of root races doesn't explain, is that as with the seventh root race, our sixth-root race designation will be a result of a developmental leap in consciousness rather than outright conquest by an outside source. This sixth root race is being born into this world at an increasing rate all the time, and it's developing within many of us already here. Yet, joining this new race is a choice that many (although probably not even half of humanity) will make.

Coming to Earth subjected almost all of our ancestors to the human condition. Everyone from all of the five root races was equally blessed with the divine gift of Free Will. Still, we were almost wiped out in our infancy. Then, as we grew up with the power of the Gods (Free Will) in our hands, we almost destroyed ourselves and the Earth in our ignorance. The good news is that it's a mistake we won't get another chance to repeat.

12

Mother Earth's Turning Points

The Earth Mother is changing her garments. She's going to put on some new stuff. She is going to be dancing around. And it's about time. She's sick and tired of the way she's been treated.

—Twylah Hurd Nitsch, medicine teacher of the
Wolf Clan, Seneca Nation

Secret Hopi legends which had been retold among their people religiously during ceremonial times since the beginning of human life on Earth were released to the world in 1979. They speak of four worldwide civilizations that existed and were destroyed before our own. They also make predictions about the ending times, which seem eerily similar to life as we know it today.

The Quero Apache speak of the same four civilizations and call what we're in now "The New Time, The Fifth World of coming together."

The Seneca call our current civilization "The Fifth World of Peace."

These last two tribes characterize our civilization as a turning point and refer to it according to its purpose—a time when we all we learn to "come together" and live in "peace" (even though we have yet to learn to do so).

∿∿∿

Ancient Aztec traditions speak of our previous civilizations as the "four Suns" (putting us in the "fifth sun" now). Each Sun described a different dawn of humanity and a different demise. According to their stories, the first period ended when the largely nomadic people, who hunted for a living, were wiped out by the animals that hunted them.

The few remaining people pulled in and started growing crops. They crossbred species, and developed Earth with their plantings until Earth reclaimed the land with tremendous winds that blew all their crops away.

The third civilization is marked by great cities and temples. Earthquakes shook them to the ground and then, just so there was no mistake as to who's in charge, it "rained fire."

During the fourth epoch, men learned to navigate the oceans. They conquered the seas! Then, the seas conquered them with the Great flood.

Do you see a pattern developing here? There's a quote by George Santayama that's carved over the entrance to the U.S. Archive. It reads, "Those who cannot remember the past are doomed to repeat it."

The past four periods, which have been virtually erased from our known history by the magnitude of their destruction, represent a huge cumulative lesson, which we wouldn't want to be "doomed to repeat." These four previous periods illustrate four of our previous primary pursuits, each having a fallback position, which became the major pursuit of the following period. Each pursuit and period carried a very pointed consequence, which confirmed that we hadn't quite gotten it right yet.

In the movie *Ghost Busters*, right before the monstrous form of the "Sta-Puft Marshmallow Man" appears, the bad guy says something like,

"Choose the form of your destroyer." In each of the four Suns or epochs on Earth, people chose the form of their destroyer by choosing a pursuit that formed the parameters of their devotion. Now that we've experienced this four times already, the question is, will we choose a devotion that is a new destroyer, or a savior this time?

The other pattern I see developing, as we finish off the four previous phases of human existence with the fifth one we're now in, is a pentagon; another holographic reminder of the five sided parameters of human experience. We use our five senses and five appendages (two legs, two arms and a head) to experience the five elements (earth, air, water, fire and ether).

The first four elements were always involved in our devotion and destruction before. The *Earth* quaked and destroyed our temples to ego, and *fire* fell from the sky. *Water* flooded the Earth, and the *air* blew away our devotion to our crops. That leaves *ether,* or Spirit, as the one element left to try our devotion on.

The number five appears everywhere with anything having to do with humans, because that is simply the number that represents the human experience of life as we know it. Now we're in the fifth and last cycle, ending in 2012 (which adds up to five, incidentally), and the pentagram stands before us as a living symbol of our relationship to nature. Also, since the fifth side of our earthly experience is in completion, I see this shape, connected to twelve others just like it is around the world and around our bodies, glowing as if they're ready to fly off. After building a firm foundation during our previous four learning experiences, we're now poised to get it right, and get on with a higher purpose.

It's really too bad that the early Church villainized the pentagram (and other symbols) which are so key to our connection to the natural world. In order to sidestep all the propaganda of satanic implications, think of it this way: Bees make hexagons in their hive, and humans make pentagons in their world. It's all about birds and bees and humans; and all the fear of the devil and the mistaken identity of his symbols have got to go before we finish this cycle.

The ancient Mayans have also clearly spelled out the nature and history of the cycles of mankind. Their explanations provide an end to those ancient stories, which the Hopi and Aztec began. It's a very convincing rendering of the human cycles and the fifth period of mankind, which ends pretty soon now. In order to know where we'll stand at the completion of this cycle, it might well be worth a close look at the object of our devotion.

This fifth period of mankind is typified by the building of that temple to human ego back in Babylon about FIVE thousand years ago. The suppressive Nefilim had left, and humans were just beginning to express their individuality. Since then, ego has taken on an infinite number of disguises. It's not just the quality of the proud hunter or the pseudo- pious temple builder anymore. In our time, ego has been endowed with an infinite number of subtle, multifaceted traps as our final test builds.

The nature of human ego has remained the same. Still, its body only grows as we continue to feed its many faces. Maybe you think you know what to do different this time so the object of your pride doesn't become your downfall again. Maybe you do, but is it possible that could just be the voice of ego you're listening to?

What do we really know, and what can we really do about it? We have our Free Will! Yet, what does that really mean, and do we really have the wisdom to use it properly now when we never have before?

When they gave Free Will to us mere mortals, it wasn't the same as the unlimited version they have in the higher worlds. It was, but it wasn't. Our karma and inclinations which are embedded in our genes and DNA usually overpowers it. What we think of as our Free Will is strongly compelled by physical factors, many of which we set up before coming here. So, by not changing any of our other realities, in effect, they gave us use of just a little of this power here on Earth and watched to see what we'd do with it. What we did with it was to almost destroy the earth—at least twice.

The first time was about 13,500 years ago on Atlantis. Shortly after being granted Free Will, thanks to Mother Earth's sympathy for the plight of the Homo sapiens, the control minded Martians living on Atlantis built a machine. They hoped this device would generate enough power to give a select few control over everyone in the world. It got out of control and all Hell literally broke loose.

Well before this, the consciousness of all the Atlanteans had been on the decline. They really worked to overcome their enlightened nature and see things in a selfish way. Thus, they severely weakened the original unity consciousness grid which had been in place since the first humanoid took up residence on Earth.

As a result of their sinking consciousness, they sank their entire continent, at least a thousand years before the great flood, and collapsed the Earth grid into our pre 1989 dodecahedronal structure. It also ripped open the bottom of their spiritual descent, affecting everyone on Earth and the Earth herself.

According to Billy, before this happened, they had crystals that would prolong youth. These were available to everyone for quite a while. As spirituality became less popular, they found a way to make this crystal power only available to a privileged few. However, the rich weren't the only ones with declining spirituality.

The Atlanteans had all been fourth-dimensional beings who seemed bent on playing follow the leader downward in consciousness for centuries. Even after their decline in consciousness, but before the accident, they had telekinesis abilities. They could move and manifest whatever they wanted, and they communicated with telepathy. However, their rulers had taken on the mission of genetically manipulating these higher qualities out of their people, just as the Nefilim did to us, so they could control them more easily.

Anger and resentment filled the air. Then, the out-of-control machine accentuated all the pent up negativity and released it with a power never before or ever again seen on this planet. The power from this accident ripped a hole in the fabric of time and space and through the membranes of the lower planes.

People plunged to the depths of the lower worlds, and the disoriented demons and lower entities came leaking fearfully though to the Earth plane. By the time the ascended masters could get most everyone back where they belonged and the rift sealed up, the consciousness of the people had dropped to the three dimensional world we've all come to know, and the stellated part of the dodecahedronal grid was totally collapsed.

This not only affected the Atlanteans but everyone on the planet. It cemented the lower consciousness of the relatively new Homo sapiens, and discouraged the Nefilim's positive involvement with the Earth and its beings even further. This physical and astral catastrophe was also like a shot to the heart of Mother Earth. Reacting like a wounded animal, she quivered and she just about died.

Her magnetism, which is a manifestation of her love to those within her vicinity, dropped to near zero for quite a while, much like a parent would withhold affection from a naughty child. As a result, all the advanced Atlantean technology and manmade objects lost their cohesiveness and vanished, so that mankind really had to start over, but with a closer connection to the Earth and their own nature.

The only manmade object on Earth that didn't vanish was the machine that the Atlanteans invented, which the Atlanteans invented which caused all the trouble. It creates its own magnetic field, so it wasn't affected by the earth's dropping magnetism. In fact, it's still running and still causing problems at the bottom of the Atlantic (in the Bermuda Triangle).

This drop in the earth's magnetism also caused most peoples' minds to lose their magnetic bond to their memories. People suddenly didn't know how to do anything; who they were, or where they were. They fell through a void of darkness for three and a half days at which time they were hit in the face with their old understanding of oneness with all things.

This is the nature of the void. An awareness of God and our unity with It is what's left when we lose attachment to anything we can perceive with our physical senses or thoughts. When the Atlanteans came out of the void, that oneness began to fade as they tried to understand how to pick up the pieces of their lives without remembering anything about the rubble around them or having any familiarity with 3-D realities.

Many of the Nefilim had protected themselves by retreating to their ship which maintained its own energy field. Those who remained on the ground were still fairly protected simply by virtue of their DNA and consciousness makeup which also generated a magnetic field around their bodies. Also, many of the relatively new Homo sapiens still had the benefits of the remnants of their parental DNA and also didn't lose their memories entirely.

Still others (Homo sapiens, Atlanteans, or others) who had been successfully stripped down to the two strand DNA we have today were able to maintain their body's energy field by use of a mind/body/"merkaba" technique. Their memories were protected to the degree they were able to create their own magnetic field. However, the vast majority simply lost their memories and went crazy to one degree or another.

That was the beginning. Mother Earth got a much needed chance to heal, and with almost nothing in their heads but a memory of the spiritual experience in the void where they knew a profound sense of unity with all things, the bulk of humanity got another chance at making better choices. However, this ignorance also made them very vulnerable to being misled.

There were three masters and a bunch of mystics, (some call them immortals) who, knowing this time would come, had completely protected their minds by generating their own magnetic fields. Like the Nefilim, many of them had better than average DNA, but many didn't too.

Mostly, these mystics lived in the Naacal School on Atlantis. The three ascended masters living on Earth flew over and picked them up, then dropped a third off in Egypt, a third off in Bolivia, and another third in the Himalayas, where Sanskrit, "the mother of all languages" was first introduced. Some of the earliest stories told in Sanskrit are of these times about the beings they knew as "gods."

Each of the three masters stayed with his third of mystics to help start civilization all over in each of the three areas. Thoth was the master who started the colony in Bolivia, and he gave them all the basics which we've come to know as the Mayan culture. He later relocated to Egypt to help things get straightened out over there. Then, he moved to Greece and planted the seeds of their golden age as the man known as Hermes.

The Nefilim who left their homes in Sumerian for the safety of their ships returned and immediately assumed their previous position as lords over the world. However, now their seat of power in the southern part of Mesopotamia (southeastern Iraq) was right next door to the Egyptian civilization started by the ascended master who went by the name of Ra.

Ra deferred to their insistence on power to keep the peace, just as the other masters did. Thus, the rulers of Sumer were allowed to coordinate the efforts of the other three areas. They had technological powers the others didn't, and since power meant so much more to them than to the others, they were allowed to have control over the world. They created order, organizing everyone's reconstruction efforts and set up a new system.

It was known that the ruling Sumerians were motivated by generally selfish interests. However, for the sake of unity, the other three areas carried out the letter of the law as the Sumerians laid it out. They did so in an enlightened and humanitarian way, hoping that the power of love and benevolence would win out. However, because of the influence of the Sumerian rulers and the collapse of the Earth grid, negativity began to get a good foothold around the world. Free Will also gave the humans a more radical, rebellious nature. So, heavy-handed negative methods were increasingly applied to keep the upstart humans in their place.

The three masters who originally ruled the three areas outside Sumer were very well-meaning. As things grew, they delegated rule to new kings who were also generally well-meaning. The highest compliment that could be paid to a king was to call him a "righteous shepherd." However, these "shepherds" increasingly treated their flock like slaves.

The original goal among the three groups set up by the ascended masters was social order and to help people reach their highest potential. They wanted to educate the masses and introduce heart oriented, right brain technologies. Still, the unity consciousness grid had collapsed, and the unruly people were quite a handful.

The three groups set up by the ascended masters planted the seeds of ancient mysticism in their areas. They really tried to lead the people back to unity awareness. However, the Sumerian leaders had different goals which sabotaged the intentions of the others.

Still, the carefully planted seeds of civilization took root, and at first, the resulting races generally grew with a sense of cooperation with each other and the Earth. These efforts changed though when egos again began to raise their ugly heads, first with the kings and then among the people. Gradually, wars began to break out, and the rulers grew even more egotistical in their roles as "gods." All these kings grew increasingly irritating to the Sumerian ET's who were really in charge.

The big discussion was about how much technology to put at the disposal of the people, and what sort of civilization would be best to set up. The civilizations in Egypt and Mexico, for instance, wanted to try to recreate a Lemurian lifestyle. They wanted to introduce all the right brain, intuitive type technology they could.

However, the Nefilim found support among many of the self-serving rulers to withhold all technology possible from the masses and treat them entirely like slaves. They made them feel grateful to be given pick axes and similar tools to make their jobs easier. To make a long story short, the wars of the gods broke out and the bad guys won.

History has been a matter of campaigns for power employing heavy-handed control and brainwashing of the masses ever since. For thousands of years, their main mass control measure was through physical intimidation. Now, the multi-strata organization of rulers, have elevated control through propaganda to an art form.

All this would seem to have little to do with Mother Earth, who was still healing. However, the story illustrates the direction that earth rulers and then the inhabitants chose to follow away from any unity awareness. That disconnection from their higher nature and other people greatly affected Mother Earth who feels what we feel.

Despite isolated stories of peaceful tribes living in harmony with the Earth for short periods of time, and enlightened rulers trying to improve the lot of the people, the general trend since the last days of Atlantis has always been toward shortsighted ego fulfillment. People made a choice during the ending times of Atlantis, and we've had to live with the consequences of that choice ever since.

This choice for ego fulfillment manifested in a very specific design pattern where certain egos rise to the top of any organization subjecting the others to their will through an intricate system of threats and rewards. From their position on the top, these rulers pull strings, unseen by the common folk who are simply steered by their reaction to the seemingly spontaneous events.

For a short while in modern society, we were also kept in line by the illusive incentive of possibly rising to the top ourselves. Personal attainment and competition has been incorporated into all of our institutions, and people have been trained to focus on the discernment and fulfillment of their personal desires.

However, even before the common folk built the pyramids, the plan has been to give the masses just enough so they don't revolt—just enough of food and shelter and just enough hope. Things have been the same pretty much everywhere since then too. Rulers fight for control of the human resource, and we pay tribute to whoever's in charge.

After the Great Flood, each of the ancient remote colonies had its own distinctions. However, the human race at that point (after the genetic manipulation and the crossbreeding of races) was a fairly homogenous group. They may not have actually spoken the same language all over the world, but they were pretty much of the same mind in their understanding of their subservient role below their rulers as beings with no real rights. This point of view is our right. However, it goes against nature and that hurts the mother of nature herself.

The next historical marker that stands out as a triumph of ego over unity consciousness took place in ancient Babylon. Ever since they erected that tower as a tribute to their egos in Babylon, people have scrambled in diverse directions, losing their awareness of their similarities to others as well as their connection to their source and to the Earth. After the aliens who ran the world as gods left, the oppressive system which they helped set up remained. Rulers were either part 'god," or pretended to be, and they went to increasing lengths to promote their own superiority.

Still, the rulers didn't do any serious damage to the Earth until WW II. As Mother Earth reached out to try to support the tortured masses with her loving energy, giving her all rendered her weak and vulnerable. The atomic bombs dropped on Japan, which brutally extinguished so much life all at once, were a shock that just about stopped her heart. Atomic testing inside the earth over the next decade, blasted her hidden reserves of life force almost into oblivion, and she almost died again in the early 1950s.

The bombs introduced an overabundance of the fire element and through her balance off to the point where her system almost entirely ceased to function. It may be hard for most to understand the killing of something that's mostly rock and water. However, a spirit lives in that body just as one dwells in our delicately balanced carbon compounds.

After her recovery in the later 1950s, she began looking for protection from her misguided children. ETs started responding, and that's why we started hearing more about UFOs after that. Better connected to her than we are, they heard her cries and rushed to her rescue.

After the war, the militaries of the world, particularly the United States and Russia, with the help of German technology, discovered the earth grid and began building bases on the energetic hubs around the world with the same ambition as the Atlanteans had—to try to control the world and everyone in it. It sounds like the stuff melodramas are made of, but it was no joke.

They discovered the Atlantean machine and tried to duplicate it, but luckily they didn't have nearly enough of the technology necessary to even fix it. Every attempt to fix that machine only made the rifts in the time/space continuum worse, and added power to the imbalance in the global energy that machine produces. If you'd listened closely during the late fifties and early sixties, and you could have heard the faint cries for help by the violated Earth.

Billy tells me that in a couple other alternative realities, our Earth did actually die. In other parts of the universe, the importance of a living, functioning Earth is much better understood than it is among Earth's own people. Beings in other parts of the galaxy, and even in other dimensions, all realize that the death of this cherished member of the galactic community would have radical implications for everyone, no matter where they lived.

People came from all over trying to help. Of course, all the attention drew some lower vibration ETs too. Unfortunately, these are the ones our governments related to best. Deals were struck, and the destructive business as usual went into warp drive with new alien technology.

Meanwhile the powerful nature of the *One Thing*, kept making steady progress with the consciousness of the people on Earth, and its disciples worked hard to reconstruct the unity awareness Earth Grid. The angelic realm never gave up on us, and communicated their inspiration to the Earth's people all throughout history. Various races also sent saviors— Buddha, Mohammad, Jesus etc. Of course all their messages got terribly corrupted after their deaths. Still, they helped uplift human perspective with their enlightening message of love and self-control.

The battle of light and dark, or individual egos versus unity conscious-ness, gathered momentum and gathered an audience from many dimen-sions from around the galaxy since the early 1950s. They were all anxious to see what humanity would do as Mother Earth approached another major turning point.

It's like a stadium with the action on Earth down in the center. Around the central attraction are hundreds of rows of seats all filled with cheering spectators. Many just want to observe us while they observe their prime directive of non-interference. Others answer prayers in small ways; while still others help enforce Galactic law to assure there won't be any more violations like the one that almost killed the Earth during WW II and at the end of Atlantis about 13,500 years ago.

One small thing they've done is to make sure that no more atomic bombs will go off at this critical juncture of Earth's evolution. I understand some tests may work, but many won't, and no atomic devises will be allowed to detonate on top of the ground any more. People in power know this too, and all the threats and scare tactics are just impotent posturing.

With the negative use of Free Will under check in this way, the power structures of our major civilizations are feeling the pressure of the rising tide of enlightened, humanitarian interests. Their powerful, supportive ET friends have abandoned them and headed back where they came from. Our rulers are grasping for power and control in inef-fectual desperation, and causing larger scale conflicts than the Earth has ever seen.

The Earth herself is also reacting to this conflict with turmoil of her own. This comes at a time when Mother Earth is due for her regular cleansing, which occurs every 13,000 years or so when she approaches a particular position in her precession around the equinox. This cleansing is necessary for physical reasons, and the purging of negativity is neces-sary for emotional/ astral reasons. Also, this time, it's especially neces-sary in order to make ascension possible.

Billy says we may lessen the catastrophes by learning to live in harmony with our Mother Earth. However, the regular purging needs to be done. Also, as the mature Mother Earth heads into her "change of life" turning point around 2013 and 2014, this cleansing is absolutely necessary. Being in harmony with Mother Earth means not fighting her or being afraid of what might happen, but joining her in our own cleansing.

~~~~~~

Grandmother Twylah was a beloved Medicine Teacher of the Seneca tribe who made her skywalk on August 21, 2007. During her memorial, Brad Steiger, who had been adopted into the Wolf Clan of the Seneca tribe, quoted some of her teachings:

> *In these final days, it is important to think of unconditional love and not to permit anything to interfere.*

Twylah believed that the Thunder Beings, or divine helpers, are now speaking to everyone, "but only the awakened Thunder People are listening."

In order to hear the Thunder Beings, she gave firm advice: "Go within...! Go within to your vital core."

> *All the great Medicine priests are saying that another time of purification and cleansing has rolled around on the great cosmic calendar. We are once again about to enter a time of earthquakes, volcanisms, and dramatic Earth changes.*
>
> *The Earth Mother is changing her garments. She's going to put on some new stuff. She is going to be dancing around. And it's about time. She's sick and tired of the way she's been treated.*
>
> *It is now time that people better get on their horses and decide which direction they're going.*
>
> *Supposing right at this moment the Earth began to quake and up in the sky world there would be thunder and lightning and so much noise that we couldn't think. The best thing that we could do for our survival would be to stand on our truth.*
>
> *Those who stand in their truth will eat whatever Mother Nature provides--and it will be roots, bark, and seeds. Before this time ends, we will be crawling on our bellies--but we will be surviving.*

People used to be much closer to nature. Now, our manmade conveniences insulate us, but a lot of that insulation is going to be torn away.

The easiest way to adapt to this coming change is to give up our attachment to that insulation.

Try standing out in nature and sending your love and support to her core. Try giving up a meal as an offering to your own clarity. Try giving up a mood. Try not resenting when nature or life takes things away.

We all have personal concerns and active egos. However, when we try to see the bigger picture, enlightened self-interest quickly makes room for the priority of peace and wellbeing for all. Remember what happened when we chose another way back on Atlantis? We opened ourselves up for over 13,000 years of reasons why that was the wrong choice.

During that time, there were some examples of the positive use of Free Will, but they were generally on the individual level. The known history of the world has been marked by one major negative use of Free Will after another. I only know of one big exception to this trend, and even that had to work with the heavy negative realities of the day to reveal the opportunity for the positive use of Free Will. When I describe what working with those realities actually meant, I'm sure I'll lose some people as they decide that unnecessary negativity entered the process.

However, just as I've finally been able to make sense out of the tragedy of my own life, it is possible to look back at the death and destruction 600 years ago in Tibet and see a positive purpose. Today, we know better than to believe that murder, especially the murder of monks, even for the best of political purposes is ever justified.

It might help you to know that those monks were well armed and died taking many of the opposition with them. It may also help to remember that "things are not always what they seem." What we come to *know* in time isn't usually what we *see* while *looking* at an event.

I tell you what: I'll just tell the story, and you can decide what's justified—or what events from that very different world simply don't benefit from our scrutiny.

13

One Positive Use of Free Will

The sounds of clashing swords and screaming men filled the air as the soldiers waited in formation for their comrades to be slaughtered in front of them. When the order was given, they charged across the Tibetan Plateau for the honor of dieing for their country, as did the next group and the next... The impermanence of physical life was a big part of their religion, and that belief channeled into their army made the ancient Tibetans a formidable opponent.

Genghis Khan didn't really want to take on these crazy Tibetans, and the Tibetans knew that mere moxie wouldn't defeat the great Kahn. So, the two agreed to meet to discuss the situation. This is significant because it's one of the first events in history to call attention to an authority figure over any of the Tibetan region.

The meeting took place up in the Tangut Empire, which is now the northwestern Chinese provinces of Gansu, Shaanxi, and Nixgxia. Genghis was conquering that area at the time, and that gave him a psychological advantage in the negotiations. It was also a safe distance from any Tibetan targets, so the Tibetans agreed.

The year was 1215 when the Khan, along with his magician and advisor (yours truly), met with Tsangpa Dunkhurwa and his six armed associates.

History records these men as "disciples," because of the religious nature of their devotion. However, they weren't really the helpless monks you might image.

Tsangpa himself was the advisor to the king of a large section of what is now Tibet. The king was just a child, so for all intense and purposes, Tsangpa was the ruler.

When the Kahn and I met with them, we allowed the seven Tibetans to keep their weapons during the discussion to make a point about our power over them, and an agreement was achieved without incident. When negotiations were complete Tsangpa and his men backed slowly out of the room and slunk back to Tibet.

Genghis verbally promised to focus his attentions elsewhere, and the Tibetans agreed to pay him a certain amount of tribute annually. This arrangement lasted until Genghis died peacefully in 1227, immediately after conquering the Tangut Empire. Historical accounts report a "mysterious disease," so I asked Billy about the possibility of foul play. However, evidently Genghis had accomplished all he needed to and basically chose to check out at the end of that cycle.

Back at home, the Tibetans continued protecting their territory the way they had always done, fiercely and very successfully. They didn't care about discomfort or even death. This unique application of detachment got them noticed. For hundreds of years, some very enlightened aliens watched and wondered about the potential of these interesting Tibetan people.

One day a herdsman came across an unusual young man up in the hills. The boy had a uniquely gentle energy. However, even if the herdsman missed that, he couldn't miss his webbed fingers and eyes that blinked from the bottom up. He carried him home on his shoulders, and they instantly deified the boy. They named him Nyatri Tsanopo, which means "chieftain seated on the throne neck."

Soon, they built him a real throne and castle, and he became the first king of the Yarlung Dynasty in 417 BC. Yarlung simply refers to the valley in which they set up this kingdom. Nyatri became the first in a long line of Tsanpos who helped prepare the Tibetans for Buddhism.

Finally, in 1391, another from his planet landed in Tibet and took up residence in a Tibetan village. He had made adjustments to his body so

he appeared more human. Still, he was immediately recognized as someone not like anyone else. They called him "Dalai", which in Mongolian
means "ocean," and "Lama," which in Tibetan is about the same as the
Sanskrit word, "guru." The ocean referred to their concept of God as "the
Ocean of Love and Mercy."

This stranger made a name for himself, and as he grew older, he introduced them to the principle of "tulku," by telling them that when he
died, he was going to come back to finish what he'd started. He told his
disciples how to recognize him, and after he died, they did as he asked.
They were surprised and delighted when they found a child who proved
to have an impossibly detailed knowledge of their beloved Dalai Lama.
They took him in, trained him to become the second Dalai Lama, and
so the tradition began.

Meanwhile, life continued as usual. Although the Dalai Lama was
teaching the people, and making differences in their personal lives, no
nationwide changes were affected until the time of the fifth Dalai Lama.
He allied with the Geluk ("yellow hat") school of Buddhism, and attacked
the rival sects of Kagyu and Joang. He also defeated the prince of Shang,
who was a secular ruler.

Establishing a new order through violent take-over was simply the
way things were done back then. The Dali Lama did this fairly easily too
after renewing his country's affiliation with the ruling Khan of the time,
"Gushi Khan." The Dali Lama wanted a broader sphere of influence, and
the Khan wanted more tribute and the claim to an Empire that went with
it. So, these two hooked up and no one could stand against them.

The rival monasteries were either closed or forcibly converted. The end
result was a united Tibet under the control of the Dalai Lama. The Khan
helped him keep enemies at bay while the Dali Lama won the religious
convictions of his people, as evidenced by their rejection of the Jesuit
missionaries who arrived in 1661 and were sent packing with almost no
converts remaining in 1745.

After his bloody rise to power, the fifth Dalai Lama began to sell the
Tibetans on the ways of peace toward the end of his life. They eventually

turned in their guns for prayer beads and applied their belief in the impermanence of life to spiritual pursuits. Instead of proving their faith on the
battlefield, they took it into mediation.

The point to this chapter (in case you were beginning to think there
might not be one) is that the Tibetans used their Free Will to abandon
their natural evolutionary path, and embrace the ways of peace. Throughout history, individuals have occasionally used their Free Will to abandon
their natural relationship with life for a higher path. However, this is the
only instance Billy and I could determine was a positive use of Free Will
by a civilization. I asked about the golden age of Greece.

"Nope." That was a natural development of their evolution (although,
it was brought to an end by the negative use of Free Will of others). All
the peaceful civilizations before the creation of Homo sapiens don't count
because they didn't even have what we know of as "Free Will." Civilizations after that were either violent or developed in a natural way and were
destroyed by the violent negative use of Free Will.

What the Tibetans did was tremendously significant. It was unprec-
edented, and an important foreshadowing of our human potential for
peace.

Normally, not many people even use Free Will. We have our nature
and prelife contracted arrangements, and the most peaceful lives usually
just tune in and stay the course. However, as we approach the dimensional shift, everyone is being pressured to use Free Will to choose one
path or another. We'll either use our Free Will to abandon our 3-D contracts and evolve with the Earth, or we'll use our Free Will to abandon
our connection to the rising vibration on Earth and insist on fulfillment
of our 3-D contracts.

Of course, many won't face that choice at all. They'll simply be allowed
to go home and wait until all the excitement is over before reincarnating
again. Making decisions about our next step is much easier on that side
where a clear view of things is a lot easier to attain. However, those who
don't check out before about 2013 will be confirming an important choice
everyday of their lives between now and when the shift finally occurs.

The assertion of our Free Will can be daunting in view of our dualistic realities. However, the Dalai Lama and modern Tibet are encouraging reminders that dramatic positive change is possible.

Between 1720 and 1911, the Tibetans allied themselves with the Manchu Dynasty of China, which protected them. Before that, two Mongol dynasties were fighting for the right to protect the Dalai Lama and Tibet. This left the Tibetans free to pursue the path of peace, which they have led ever since.

When China attacked Tibet in 1959, brutally murdering the helpless Tibetans, the Dalai Lama simply walked away. He moved with about 80,000 Tibetans down to India, and this peaceful retreat secured his claim to the higher moral ground. He's met with the Pope many times since then, and in 1989, the same year the unity awareness Earth Grid was complete, he was recognized for the completion of his mission with the Nobel Peace Prize.

The Dalai Lama has grown to be the symbol of the heart of Tibet, and that heart has only been getting stronger ever since he first appeared in 1391. Today, he and Tibet stand for peace and harmony, and they stand out as examples of how the peaceful way of life can survive in a violent world. They give the rest of us hope and a vision of a better way, at a time in our planetary evolution when that vision is critical.

This new vision complicates things. Suddenly, nothing is as simple as it once was. It's harder to believe in the total evilness of our enemies, and MUCH harder to believe in the total virtue of our leaders...Now, the emerging vision is that there is an unbreakable bond of love between us and everyone else. We can see the whole universe as a single entity. This changes everything! And there are many who aren't quite ready for EVERYTHING to change.

14

The Gift of New Sight

> *We are in the most significant evolutionary transition*
> *that our species has ever encountered. There is no way to*
> *compare what we are now experiencing with anything in*
> *our past. This new event has no historical antecedent. The*
> *only event in the history of our species that compares with*
> *this one is Genesis.*
>
> —Gary Zukav

When the master lens workers finally finished the energetic, crystalline grid in 1989, everyone on Earth got a new pair of prescription glasses. Looking through the new stellated caps takes a little getting used to. We used to see action just fine, and we got used to thinking we knew what it meant. However, this new sight makes the reality of the action clear for anyone who wants to focus on it. Where we saw shadows, now we can see the luminous essence behind those shadows. Where we used to look for hope, now we can see the reasons for that hope.

Spiritual masters throughout the ages have told us about the enlightened view of things. Still, that vision generally led to a very difficult path. The negative power really had a pretty firm hold on things. To ignore that fact usually carried some dire consequences. It's okay to admit that now. That was reality! However, now all that has changed.

With the completion of the new grid, the forces of light have actually achieved dominance in this world. The grid isn't only a supporter of consciousness. It's a reflection of it. It uses us to build itself, and we use it to build ourselves—both drawing from the *One Thing* at the core of it all. If our harmony with the forces of light which draw their power from the *one* real *thing* in the universe weren't stronger than our affinity to the opposing forces, the new grid wouldn't have been completed. Our collective consensus of reality sustains it, just as IT helps sustain that consensus.

With this solid platform for unity consciousness, we now have a much more appealing choice in front of us. Many still struggle to see things the way they've always known them to be. They prefer the familiarity of reliance on their five outer senses (and the unseen sense of reactive judgment) to their new sense of perception.

However, this new, increasingly popular sense of perception is safe now, and it's getting safer all the time as more people discover it. It's also vital to our evolution. Without it, the grid would be weakened. The more people rely on it, the more the new grid gets reinforced. with our expectations.

So, this new sight is safe, necessary and it's easy. Seeing all the beautiful new colors is as simple as shifting our attention away from what our mind thinks we're seeing and onto the depth and wealth of what our heart knows.

Of course, we still have the Free Will to choose what we see and what we don't. Also, knowing what we're seeing, after looking at a blurry world for so long, isn't automatic. Yet, that is where our hope lies.

This new vision complicates things. Suddenly, nothing is as simple as it once was. It's harder to believe in the total evilness of our enemies, and MUCH harder to believe in the total virtue of our leaders. That's the curse of seeing the dimensions of a person instead of just a single aspect of the figures.

It was much easier when we knew who the bad guys were. It was so much simper when we knew our special place in opposition to all the evilness in the world. Of course, it's always much easier to be wrong than right.

Now, the emerging vision is that there is an unbreakable bond of love between us and everyone else. We can see the whole universe as a single entity. This changes everything! And there are many who aren't quite ready for EVERYTHING to change.

Millennia ago, this unity consciousness grid had been firmly in place since the dawn of time. However, the power of individual ego chose to see a reality which was more suited to their interests than the natural one everyone else saw. People wondered about this and tried to see if they could see things the way those with all the personal successes did.

Suddenly, masses of individuals were focused on themselves so much that they couldn't see the One life anymore. They couldn't see their connection with others. The Universe responded to this by collapsing the grid so it was easier to see things the way everyone wanted. The prism cap that made the world sparkle with wonder and interconnected love was simplified into the linear plane of human ego. Thus, we created God in our own image, and we were thereafter much freer to see the world any way we personally wanted.

Humanity was young and rebellious. We got into trouble, and we've been learning from that ever since. It took a while to turn things around, but the proof of the lesson is the new grid which is a gift of new vision for all of us. Just as kids often grow to see things the way their parents do, we're finally growing to see things the way our ancient ancestors did. Many of us, at least, are trying to give up our childish ways. We're trying to see and consciously appreciate unity with our family.

We've all been alone too long! Life on our own hasn't always been as rewarding as we had hoped when those selfish urges set in. In fact, many millennia of trying it that way, one mistake after another, has left many of us more than ready to rejoin the fold. We've worked in cubicles, isolated ourselves at home, transferred away from friends and family, and cut ourselves off from everyone else in every imaginable way, all for the sake of ambition. I grew up thinking that's how things were supposed to be.

Prejudices make this belief easier. Looking for ways to reassure ourselves that we're better than anyone else, and deserve what we personally want for our lives while others don't, really helps justify selfishness. You start by looking for obvious differences such as skin color, sex, language, or political differences.

I remember when I was a kid during the Cuban missile crisis. One day, I was in a car full of my fellow boy scouts, and our leader, who was driving the car, said with great resolve, "If those dirty commies ever took over this country, I'd kill my family and myself rather than have to live under their rule."

Spoken like a true patriot! Even as a kid, I knew something was wrong with this guy.

After millions of years living in every setting possible, something inside just isn't comfortable with these egotistical generalizations. Personally, I remember living as a member of every race on Earth (and then some). I remember lives as a woman, a man, and a gay man. I remember being a warrior, and a wuss, a priest, a poet, a catholic, and a pagan; being royalty, and fighting against royalty. I remember being a magician, who controlled people; and I remember many, many lifetimes being controlled. It's hard to be prejudice against someone who could have been you in a different time and place.

Fear also helps hold personal, selfish ambition in place. Good becomes bad. The personal ambition to rise above the common masses becomes good. Everything it takes to hold the vision of our personal success in place becomes good, and any inefficient distractions have to be quickly dealt with. Friends, family, coworkers often fall into this category, and so the sun rises and sets on another day in the dog-eat-dog world.

For many thousands of years, everyone experienced this in one way or another and that habit doesn't change overnight. No matter how common someone actually is, they always want to rise above their peers in one way or another. To really be efficient with those ambitious goals, we need to try to look through the linear lens of our own making.

In the last few hundred years, this lens has been aggressively applied in all walks of life. Profit motives have replaced human ones. A new morality has emerged that says that a corporation's primary (translate "primary" as "only") responsibility is to their stockholders. A lawyer's only responsibility is to his client. The government's only responsibility is to its own people and to maintain their way of life (and the governments hold on them) at any cost. Human values are angrily disregarded with prejudiced-laced propaganda and primitive protective rhetoric.

Yet, the government isn't the enemy, and the enemy they focus on certainly isn't the enemy. The conflict is simply between our old vision of the world and our new one. Thanks to the world of big problems, we don't have to look through a magnifying glass to see this anymore.

The issue is right in front of us "big as life." Still, the choice of what we see is up to us. The new sight allows us to see our interconnectedness with a friendly universe more clearly. Or some (maybe reps from government, religions, or any large establishment) could see this new friendliness as a formidable obstacle in their way of playing on our prejudices and egos to justify our superiority over others so they can keep their power plays going. They use phrases like, "the greatest nation in the history of the world," or "God's chosen people." However, many are seeing through all that now.

These groups constantly bless us by making our choice really simple. Despite all the appearances of all the different choices, what it comes down to is the choice of using power over others for the sake of our own ego, or choosing love with the good of the whole in mind.

The old vision would see this as a choice between our desires and the rights of others. The new vision knows it's not about who deserves what, or about giving up anything! **It's simply a matter of expanding our understanding of our own enlightened self-interest to include blessings for all.**

~~~

The conventional wisdom of the old vision dictates that we all must compete for the limited resources at hand. However, looking through the new lens, we can see that working cooperatively with the Universe will result in more secure, peaceful prosperity than we could ever have accumulated working by ourselves on our own selfish goals.

The dawning reality in this new light is that it's not about good guys versus bad guys, or the rich against the poor, or even the wise and righteous against the ignorant and wrong. We're all divine beings, pretending to be what we know as human. The big distinction between people, which is forming a more distinct division in our world all the time, is whether we choose to see the world through the new unity consciousness lens, or to dig in our heels and see things the way we've always seen them throughout the known human history.

I covered a lot of this history briefly in the previous chapter mainly to illustrate the ramifications of the latter choice. The many millennia of murder and mayhem, the battles for constant control over each other where everyone looses, all can be traced back to that seemingly innocent decision to justify the promotion of personal interests over the universal good.

Not everyone was around for all of that, and each divine being still has that divine quality of Free Will to use as they see fit. I just wanted to point out that I see a gift associated with unity conscious awareness which wasn't available before. Finally, after over 13,000 years, the choice to be a nice guy isn't the choice to always finish last. Soon, nice guys are going to find themselves in a race all their own.

15

Divergent Views (The Problem)

Working to harmonize with the divergent views around us just makes us better people. It makes us patient, flexible, and humble. However, sometimes views diverge to a point where they just aren't compatible anymore. People go their own way, and we finally get a break from those irritating, personal lessons for a while.

Our Mother Earth has been a great sport. She volunteered to be the home of dualistic beings during the Free Choice experiment. She knew full well, that the experiment could have dire consequences for her. She volunteered for the mission because of her love for life and her faith in that love. However, after that last assault on her life which started with WW II, Mother Earth sent out a prayer to be rescued from the dangers of 3-D reality.

The ascended masters had been rebuilding the unity consciousness grid by working with human attitudes and consciousness for the last 13,000 years. The rising consciousness of humanity eked out support of these efforts and allowed the project to make slow progress. However, just a few hundred years ago, the masters didn't know if they'd finish on time.

If mankind was of the same mind as we were before the fall of Atlantis, our intent would have sabotaged this unity awareness project, and we'd probably have died with the Earth. However, as it is, the grid project was finished in plenty of time, and people have been reinforcing it ever since to the dismay of the pretenders who run world affairs.

Another factor working to stimulate discord and divergent views ever since that catastrophe on Atlantis has been the machine they invented. Neither the Atlanteans, nor anyone who has discovered it since, have ever been able to turn it off. It still sits off the Atlantic coast in what is called the Bermuda triangle. Besides occasionally causing trouble for the ships which pass over it, this machine regularly sends out low level disharmonic energy which has been muddling minds with unnecessary conflict for over 13,000 years now. It's been said to have contributed to the escalation of issues that have caused mental confusion, relationship conflicts, wars, and all sorts of radical reactions throughout our known history.

"Wars and rumors of wars" have added to the emotional tension of divergent views. Some people react with love and compassion, while others react by pulling in their unity networking feelers and maybe even plotting a counter attack. World leaders have fostered divergent views and tension to keep us off balance and easier control. However, we're increasingly developing immunity to these tactics.

Today, whenever there's a catastrophe, whether man made or natural, prayers and love for the fallen victims reinforces the grid. Whenever we react with compassion for those who appear to be under the control of oppressors, the positive forces are strengthened. Those trying to put the squeeze on people find that their control is slipping right between their fingers, even if all their victims don't. All in all, these wielders of the old power are finding they're losing the battle.

This heart connection for those in trouble has powered up the grid of unity consciousness, which in turn has inspired many more to rely on it further. This reliance on unity awareness has propelled our consciousness, and that of the Earth, way past any reasonable hopes that the masters who began the reconstruction project originally had!

Billy tells me that the ascended masters didn't fix the grid with any expectations for us in mind. "They just did what they could do and left the rest up to you."

I'll bet a lot of our spectators had expectations though. I can just see them taking bets in the stands. Billy did confirm that all the cheering fans around the Earth plane have helped us strengthen the new grid with their love and enthusiastic support. In a world where thoughts are things, their emotional/psychic support has translated into real reinforcement for the new grid and its allies.

This project has been so successful that those of us who have helped support unity awareness have helped uplift mankind and Mother Earth to a point where it soon won't even be compatible with three dimensional realities anymore. This was discovered in 1997 and confirmed in 1998, nine years after the completion of the grid. Suddenly, a new, higher vibratory place had to be prepared for our evolution, and it's under construction right now. Billy says I've been there, but we can't stay because it's not entirely solid yet.

At any rate, this evolution to a new dimension is a tremendous success! However, it also carries a small dilemma. Despite the tremendous extent of our divergent views here on Earth, everyone has remained physically compatible, so far. Now, the Earth and many of its people are scheduled for ascension to a place that's not compatible with the three dimensional realities that many others are not yet ready to give up.

This is the home of Free Will—"the home of the free and land of the brave." We were promised Free Will. Many brave souls have gotten very involved and attached to this place and aren't ready to move on quite yet. On the other hand, many other brave souls, along with the Earth herself, have put up with a lot over the eons and ARE ready to move on.

The Universe loves us and isn't about to change the Free Will rules mid stream. In other words, It can't simply hold those back who deserve and wish to move on. Nor can it move people against their will (even to a place many of us would consider better), when those people have signed up for long term contracts on the 3-D Earth and have confirmed their desire to fulfill those contracts.

There are many people who aren't ready to defer to the good of the whole if it means compromising their personal goals. They'll have to learn the same as we did. That takes time. Also, Billy told me that there are new souls being born all the time. Up until recently, these new souls were conceived with 3-D realities in mind, and contracted into that reality.

The Universe isn't a deal breaker. It is, however, infinitely creative. What do you do with two groups of humans who suddenly have incompatible hopes, expectations, and needs? The solution to that dilemma is beyond the imagination of most of us mere mortals.

In fact, even now that this solution is a solid plan, the belief in that solution is probably also beyond most people. Like the ancient mariners who thought that if you sailed too far you'd fall off the edge of the earth, many will say that this solution simply isn't possible. However, isn't trying to extend our awareness past its limits with assertions of what isn't possible just another reaction of ego?

Some may agree the solution is possible. However, very few will really know... We may be the students and even teachers in this school of physical life, but it's a good thing someone else is in charge of maintaining the ground on which it rests.

16

The Origins of Life

Life isn't about finding yourself. Life is about creating yourself.

—George Bernard Shaw

Before we get into the solution to the dilemma of the divergent goals within our race, let's talk about where we all came from. The idea of "new souls," which was brought up in the last chapter, was a new concept for me. I guess I thought we all started about the same time.

"On your mark, get set, go!" With that, the gates of heaven opened, and we were all off and flying in different directions for all we were worth.

However, when I asked where these new souls came from, Billy answered: "You create them."

"What? How?"

"It just takes a thought," he replied with a knowing smile and that silence, which has taught me so much!

My guides worked with my imagination for weeks to slowly and ponderously unveil the mechanics of this creation process, which was later verified through Billy. The first thing I realized was that new souls, like all things, are created from the *One Thing*. As I tried to imagine examples of how a thought might create a new soul, it occurred to me that this creative love could take on all sorts of disguises, depending on whose dream it is and what they wanted to accomplish. This thought bloomed into a surprising discovery, but not before I first explored alternative lives.

Billy confirmed that alternative lives often take on a life of their own. So if "life is about creating yourself," as George B says (above), that's certainly an interesting way to do it. Still, that's not really a way to create a completely new soul.

When we come to important crossroads and put out a strong wish that we could go both ways, a part of us actually takes the path we didn't choose. Usually, we'll let go of that decision at some point, and cut that alternative self loose to begin life of its own. However, that doesn't create the blank slate of a new soul, and it doesn't always work this way.

In my case, I'm really invested in my two major alternative lives. I stay in touch with them and sometimes feel their successes and failures. The two of us who are still in the physical world (myself and that alternate life as the professor) will meet up with the one who passed away a couple years ago, and we'll eventually merge back into our higher self and happily share all the experiences.

However, as I mentioned, even when an alternative life continues along a path that we totally abandoned, its still not exactly a "new soul". This new life, which sprouted from a fork in the road of life, really just adds another dimension to "creating yourself." When we put enough energy into a choice not made, we actually make it on some level. That creates an alternative self and, in a sense, a new self, but not a totally new soul.

I asked if the two other manifestations of me living in the Ukraine and in India were new souls. Nope. They're just other manifestations of me too. They're simply gathering different experiences in a different location. When those lives are finished, we'll also merge again into one.

~~~~

Creating a new soul is like creating an alternative life, except that it generally results from our thoughts and feelings around what we perceive as the need to accomplish the impossible. A fork in the road may result in a wish that leads to an alternative life. However, when we want something that doesn't seem to be possible anywhere on our road, that's when the miracle of new life can occur.

Nature doesn't like impossible situations. Perceived needs are filled, one way or another. Perhaps our higher self will pick up on our desire and manifest another body to explore it. However, if it doesn't deem that desire necessary for its fulfillment, and if our desire is strong enough, our thoughts and prayers can create a new soul who'll manifest in a new situation to fulfill that desire. In other words, when we're resolute in a desire that we can't imagine ourselves ever satisfying, the energy of that desire can actually manifest a new soul, and the motivation of the desire will give that new soul its initial purpose for life.

Although we don't usually think of things this way, this function is observable and it is within the human ability to *know* how it works. With that said, I'm going to continue relay this process as I see it:

Since people can face their hopeless situation in a positive or negative way, they'll either harbor positive or negative desires. It follows that positive, constructive desires would manifest a new soul with an optimistic slant on life. Similarly, negative, destructive desires resulting from a reaction to a hopeless situation will manifest a negatively inclined soul.

Have you ever wondered why some people are so sure that people are basically good, while others are convinced that our nature is negative? It's because of their basic orientation and possibly because of the way they were originally conceived. A new soul can come into being with either primary tendency.

～～～

However, once on the ground, nature begins to bring the force that's lacking into balance. We're all created from the *One Thing*...the same God stuff. Still, the starting spots in this world can vary in extremely opposing ways. Since thoughts, wishes and hopes can be so divergent; their creations are going to equally diverse.

Whether you actually create a new soul or just send some unstructured energy into the ethereal realm, depends on how much of the *One Thing*—the creative, energy—you put into it. If you were creating something negative, you wouldn't think of it as being created out of the loving energy of the *One Thing*. Still, the source of all desires and the means for their fulfillment all come from the same place. All desires are really the desire for completeness (God) and love in disguise, and all creative energy is a result of that urge.

Even if someone dreams about being a bad guy, that dream is in the hopes that it will bring that person balance and happiness. Once a soul starts living that life, it will learn and have other dreams and goals. No matter what people think they want, or what they think they're creating, it comes from the one raw source, and if it manifests at all, sooner or later, it all evolves into a more consciously loving entity.

The first example I thought of to explain how this creation of a new soul could happen I call *creation by default*. In other words, if your desire for an experience can't find any other outlet, it's going to create one all by itself. For instance, I'll bet somewhere out there, there's a poor woman who feels powerless and dreams of a life of power and wealth.

If she imagined herself getting from here to there, her dreams would probably somehow manifest in her own life or future life. Or these dreams could also possibly lead to an alternative life. Or, they may remind her of a past life from which she could internalize that experience. The dreams could also put her in harmony with someone from her past or someone in her soul family presently living somewhere else in the world that is well to do or powerful. However, if the energy of her dreams doesn't lead her to someone already in existence somewhere in time and space, that energy has to go somewhere. So it manifests as a new soul with a particular intent, but not much else.

The bottom line here is that if she puts energy into leading a life of power and wealth to which she can't personally relate in any possible way, she'll actually create that being. Given enough energy, this dream being will eventually be born into a life with a contract to acquire power and wealth. This was the first scenario that occurred to me since I see so many people in the world now with power and wealth who look like they must be new, inexperienced souls.

People can be dissatisfied with life for a variety or reasons, and whenever they feel like there's no possible way to get from where they are to the life they dream about, and they aren't open to experiencing it vicariously through another, that dreaming energy begins the process of creating a new soul who will be born to live that dream. It would be a much more responsible and efficient use of that creative energy to visualize yourself leading the life you want. If people could only see where all their creative energy goes, they might have more faith in it.

Realizing this, it occurred to me that those with the most lack of faith probably do most of the creating of new souls. That's an interesting conclusion in light of the fact that most people believe the most powerful of all beings (God) is the only one who can create new souls. For me, this is another comforting reminder that for one reason or another, most people are simply wrong about how all the important stuff works. Could that be because our creator originally put us here with a fairly simple purpose?

Creation from the ground up by the workers on the ground seems like the natural order of things to me. That's how construction as we know it works. Why would the construction of mankind be any different?

I think it's also tremendously significant that life as we know it is created, for the most part, by the least of us. This discovery in itself literally elevates the hopeless masses to the status of the creators of the known universe. They are the moving parts in the machine that perpetually recreates our world! It's a humbling realization, which tends to equalize the importance of everyone around us.

On the other hand, looking at how an advanced soul handles life brings up another interesting of process, which might be considered the creation of a new soul (but actually isn't). A dear member of my soul family once told me that she was once part of Merlin. I contemplated this for quiet a while before realizing what had happened.

We all have guides who stick around and watch from a distance, helping out when they can. Other souls often come around too and help when they feel inspired, and they sometimes stick around if they enjoy relating to that individual and his or her experiences. If a person has a particularly powerful purpose and life path, a wandering soul may be invited to blend with that person for a while. The wandering soul will add a new talent or enhanced awareness to the person in trade for experiencing his or her life.

Merlin was originally one man who had a particularly positive and powerful path. Souls were drawn to him and invited to stay to enhance the life that others knew as Merlin. When I asked how many blended into this one soul experience, I was told it was so many that the number was unimportant. Merlin became a one-man culture. Like all cultures, it eventually disbanded, piece by piece, soul by soul. Thus, this conglomerate of souls was not a new soul but more of a cooperative venture, which held together as long as it needed to. It also shows how an advanced soul will conserve creative energy, channeling it in personally beneficial ways, which may seem magical to anyone else.

When enough imaginative energy is put into a dream, that energy manifests and eventually finds its way to Earth. Dissatisfaction isn't the only motivating factor. People put energy into dreams they can't personally relate to (and therefore get to) for a variety of reasons. A simple, natural, playfulness might be equally creative.

Picture an innocent child who is still connected to the angelic realm. He or she might have imaginings that could lead to the creation of simple and pure creatures such as fairies. When I think of the nature of fairies, I can see how the power of a child's laugh fed through his or her simple, wandering mind could result in the creation of such a being.

Of course, this same principle would explain how an angry heart could create new demonic souls. This is what happened during the Atlantean period before the fall. People would imagine an evil entity doing things they couldn't imagine doing themselves. Then, when that machine tore open the rift, they met their children, or their enemy's children. Many of these new souls easily found harmonious hosts and moved right in.

There's a moral to that story about being careful about your passions and imaginings. No one really wants to admit the possibility of that his or her secret thoughts actually manifest. However, try to look surprised about the moral. The fact that you can't should tell you something. Secret thoughts just don't stay secret very long.

They all add to our marvelously diverse universe sooner or later. Just as beautiful, playful fairies have a place in the world that's separate from most human experience, so do demons. They also have a place specially designed to match their particular needs and learning process. It's not Hell. It's not a punishment. Like all life, they are on their way to discovery of their own divine nature in their own particular way.

The second way we can create new souls isn't really by default, but it's still usually an accident. An example occurs to me as I watch Lilly, my wife's ever-present cat. Billy confirmed that Lilly used to be Guinevere, my wife's faithful dog. When Guinevere died, she was reborn as Lilly.

Generally, the contract animals make before entering the physical world is pretty simple. It specifies what kind of animal they'll be and their general way of life. Like a human, Guinevere/Lilly came in with a lot more. For one thing, she came with a contract to find Danna again.

Lilly acts like a dog, following her everywhere. When Danna's not around, she follows me everywhere. She doesn't really seem like a normal cat OR dog to me. She seems to have lost most of her cat nature and often looks a little confused or at loose ends—kind of like a human. I think a lot of pets might be like this.

People often put so much creative love into their pets that they actually create something that wasn't originally there. I used to think of this as a consciousness enhancement for the cat or dog soul. However, the more I think about it, the more I believe that the creative, expectant thoughts some people direct toward their pets actually creates a new life—a new soul that lives within the consciousness of the pet as long as that pet is alive.

I know there will be many who say that only God can create new souls. That was my assumption too just a couple weeks ago. However, we have to remember two things. First of all, "God" really is the fallback explanation when we're not aware of the real reason for something we observe. God used to be the reason the sun rose in the morning and set in the evening. So we have to keep our minds open to the actual mechanics of things.

The other thing that's good to remember is "as above so below." If God can create souls, why can't we? Principles that work in heaven work here the same way. That's the basis of all alchemical answers and the whole point to the miraculous magic of life!

Maybe the story of our creator was a story of someone just like us. That's sort of a scary thought. However, it also speaks volumes about our potential.

Like God, people can create souls on purpose. However, life is so full of opportunities to use our creative energy to help get through our own personal challenges that I think most souls are probably created the other way. Just as trees create life-giving oxygen as a byproduct of their growth, humans create new souls as a byproduct of moving through their lives. Both are a necessary addition to the world.

〜〜〜

Actually, the world makes a bigger spot for new souls than most realize. Whenever there is an opportunity for a soul to live a life on earth, that void is filled. For instance, back on Atlantis, they manipulated genes much like our scientists are doing today. They created strong men with low intelligence to use as beasts of burden. They gave them the head of a bull or something else not human to remind everyone that these were not people, and therefore didn't have a soul. They called them "things."

They made other "things" for other uses too, claiming their inventions for their own, much like our corporate researchers are doing today with lower life forms. They assume that since they manipulate cells and genes a unique way, which God never has before, that their creation is theirs to own.

The first assumption, that we can actually "own" anything, especially another life form, is another delusion of ego. The next assumption they made was that what they created didn't have a soul. Wrong again. They created an opportunity for life, and nature filled it. Given the slightest opportunity, nature will always move in!

As is generally the case today, their assumption was that only humans have a soul, so we can do whatever we want with the rest of life we find or create. Strike three; mistake upon mistake upon mistake!

Generally, the most enlightened people back then, who allowed for the possibility that the "things" might have a soul, consoled themselves much the same as those today who justify using specially bred animals for experimentation, while being shocked by the use of other animals for this torturous purpose. I suppose the reasoning goes like this: "If this being has any consciousness, it knew what it was getting itself into before in came to Earth, and therefore is getting what it bargained for."

Actually, I see another possibility as much more likely. What if these sweet beings contracted to allow themselves to be put into that position to give us an opportunity to experience compassion and save them? In a world designed to teach love, a selfless act such as that by "man's best friend" actually seems like a pretty good possibility to me.

∿∿∿

What genetic researchers and experimenters on animals don't realize is that consciousness is the skeleton on which the body of life is built. You can't create a living body without consciousness entering it to give it inner structure! In fact, taking this one step further, all life, even inanimate life such as in rock or the Earth, has a sacred consciousness of which we need to be aware so we don't violate its sanctity.

Another example of how to create a new soul has been exemplified with movies like *I Robot* (with Will Smith), and *Renaissance Man* (with Robin Williams). If someone creates a robot out of non-organic tissue with artificial intelligence, which can function in the world just like a human, is it possible for that robot to have a soul just like a human? Absoposolutely! No question about it.

Eventually, it all comes back to the one living thing. Consciousness is everywhere we look, and it's only human ego that denies that fundamental fact. Life creates life as we evolve to a more enlightened place. A big part of that evolution is learning to recognize and appreciate the sanctity of the life all around us.

Not all life, even human life, is all that evolved. What people actually can see varies, and Free Will leads us in many divergent directions. It's hard to phantom the diverse directions a good, constructive life can take. Yet, given enough energy, the Universe can and does bring any dream to life one way or another.

It brings dreams to life within the dream of life, and constantly brings new characters into that dream. Whatever the dream, the characters in it are eventually led to the lesson of love, which is the whole purpose of life. Whether we personally dream about Heaven or Hell, seriousness or fun, responsible or un…we're all eventually heading for the same place—a place all souls, no matter how different, can call home.

17

The Triumph of Free Will (The Solution)

Education is the path from cocky ignorance to miserable uncertainty.

−Mark Twain

First of all, it's important to understand that we don't have to ever entirely understand everything. Understanding (according to Hunt) is only useful when it makes us more comfortable with knowing ourselves and our place in the world. THE important thing to remember is that we're working with an infinitely creative Universe, which WILL eventually give everyone what they need. That's the premise, and it works because the singular principle in the Universe draws on an infinite amount of the *One Thing* to make ANYTHING possible.

Here we are, sitting on an Earth, which has used her Free Will to opt up and out of the 3-D experience. To this end, many of us, and beings from other worlds, are cooperating with her. Our energy and optimism helps reinforce the new grid, and the intent of our practical steps helps ease Mother Earth and humanity through this change. The sun, which is like the mother of our Mother Earth, is also working with her.

The whole universe is cooperating, and as a result, this new energy and awareness is shaking up social, political and economic institutions. Enlightenment is sprouting under their foundations. It's breaking them up, and there's not much anyone can do about that besides go down kicking and screaming.

The Earth is going through a cleansing; human institutions are going through a cleansing, and people are discovering their priorities in the process. Earth changes help displace or confirm our old mindsets in a number of ways. Watching what our leaders do or don't do when faced with human tragedy shows their real priorities. Similarly, all of us will be faced with choices, which force us to rely on our old limited mindsets or open ourselves up to new trust-based ones.

Many will also grow in unity consciousness as they take more responsibility for their community when public services fail us. Others will hold up and horde, keeping neighbors at bay at gunpoint. Many will open up to new, more humanitarian priorities, while others hang onto the old familiar ones.

The really interesting part about the developing solution is how Nature is preparing to bring about a better world for ALL humans while our population is rapidly diverging into two camps. We have the new souls with 3-D contracts, people with a vested interest, and others who, for one reason or another, will want to keep operating in the 3-D world they've come to know. Then we have all those who wish to evolve with Mother Earth to a place that's totally incompatible with 3-D realities.

Both groups of spiritual beings have the divine use of Free Will. The universe can't hold one back or push the other ahead. Free Will dictates that all humans can pick their own perspective.

After two near death experiences, Mother Earth is evolving out of here. It's not even a difficult decision that might result in an alternative life, which could conceivably maintain the status quo. After many millions of years of service to mankind, our Mother is moving on with her full presence dedicated to the new life in front of her.

Many of us will be evolving with her. That seems simple enough. However, what about the souls who don't want to move on? I've read that they will move to sister planet.

Yet, when I asked Othello of the Ashtar Command about this, he said, "There is no other dualistic world that has Free Will. You're unique! That was the great experiment." Actually, that's what started all the thought and discussion about Free Will a few chapters back.

At any rate, if people couldn't move to a similar/sister planet and they couldn't stay here, I couldn't see any answer. However, Othello told me the answer, and it's been confirmed by Jesse and Billy now on many occasions. He said, "Your Earth will split."

When I asked Jesse and Billy about this, they said the same exact words. All three explained what I explained above about divergent views, our evolution and the changes here on Earth. However, they were silent about what exactly an "earth split" meant. Over time, I figured it out, and they confirmed my thoughts as they always do with concepts that are new to me before I go public with any of it.

Evidently, although what's about to happen has never happened before in the infinity of time and space, it is occurring using natural laws which have always been in place. It's never happened before because there was never a dualistic world with Free Will before, let alone one that was evolving out of the 3-D reality. However, now that we're to this point, the natural laws of love and manifestation are simply called into action. They'll be applied as never before. Still, it's all part of the spiritual system and natural reality we're all just beginning to understand.

Just as we can create new souls individually, we can also create them collectively. People who cling to their old 3-D way of looking at things strongly enough will resist the pull of ascension with the Earth. Their expectations that one day will be just like the previous one will actually manifest that reality. Their wishes and expectations (powered by divine Free Will) will actually create a new soul, which will look just like the earth they've always known.

Many souls, old and new, will want to finish their contracts on the 3-D Earth—an Earth that's scheduled to depart from the 3-D realm of reality. Yet Free Will is a divine, creative force. In this case, expectations will trigger this creative Free Will power into manifesting a miracle which will prove their expectations true. Thus, the story of the 3-D Earth will continue as it always has—with lots of power and lots of misconceptions.

Just like the evolved Earth is already created but not solid enough to move into yet, the new 3-D world is also already a reality on a subtler plane. After the Earth ascends, those left behind will be able to stand their ground and say, "See, nothing is changing..." As they look out at the world they just manifested to validate their own illusion, they'll feel confident in their resolve that the world is still the same!

Actually, it won't quite be the same under the surface of things. The new earth will have the vitality of youth and the happy resolve that comes with youth and no desire to be anywhere but in the third dimension. Also, at the time of the split, everyone on both planets will have much better use of improved DNA, which makes them more capable to leading a better and longer life. If the 12-strand DNA isn't manifested physically (which is a good possibility), it still will be more accessible because of our higher vibrations and closer proximity to the subtle plane in which it exists.

Both worlds will also have better leaders in place. At this writing, there's a lot of concern about our leadership and consequently, our future. Many things are happening that make normal people feel very vulnerable and helpless. However, we are being looked after. In this case, Mother Earth is going to emerge as our savior.

Currently, all the major countries have been building huge underground cities for decades in order to protect the corrupt governments of the world. After their remote viewers saw these cities crumbling many years ago, they began making them much stronger, reinforcing the already reinforced concrete with 4-inch-thick seamless stainless steel. By all the known science, these encampments should be just fine no matter what hits them. Some of their own people foresee problems, but they must be wrong because according to all the simulations, these fortresses are simply indestructible!

However, this is just another instance where things are not what they seem. Billy tells me very few will actually emerge from those elaborate cities, which have usurped the world's resources for so long now. Evidently, these people and their plans just aren't in harmony with the earth.

Our Mother Earth is an intelligent being who is going to take care of things before she ascends. Some good people will make it out of those underground cities. However, the plans to pick up rule where the holed up authorities left off before all the destruction will never materialize. Too many of their numbers will have perished in the tombs they created as strongholds.

However, leadership will emerge quickly as many genuinely concerned people, who are being positioned right now, follow their hearts and move into action. Many of the new leaders on the 3-D world will be people who are of a like mind with the 3-D humans. Others will set systems up and train people so things will proceed better after they move on with the evolving Earth. Still other leaders, who could go, will choose to remain behind to help.

Besides these two destinations, many on the Earth will go other places when they die just as they've always done. There are countless worlds that are appropriate for taking the next step for many individuals. There are also lower forms of life available for souls who've misused their Free Will.

This is a situation other dualistic worlds don't have. No one elsewhere ever has to transmutate into a lower life form because no one has ever had Free Will to abuse. Basically, the way it works is that if you abuse your Free Will by usurping the Free Will of others, you come back and learn how that feels so you won't do it again. You do penance and confirm your new understanding.

There is (or was, anyway) a misconception among black magicians that if they totally cut themselves off from the constructive input of their higher self or other benevolent influences, that they'll be immune to those painful lessons, which would otherwise guide them back to the light. That much is true. However, their error lies in the fact that there is only one power in the Universe. Since there is no opposite power in which to take refuge, their strategy isn't the final answer they believe it to be.

No matter how carefully someone cuts himself off from his higher self while living, when he finally loses conscious grip on things as his physical body dies, his higher self, once again calls the shots. New souls who are negatively oriented may be given a little leeway. However, when the time is right, the over-soul or higher self, who is by nature a balanced soul (never overly committed to a negative path), will intervene.

If this person who used Free Will to trample the rights of others has no inclination to ever open up to the ways of the heart, the higher self has no other alternative but to remove temptation from that soul's path. That soul, who has moved past all the options to learn a more humane way of living, is relocated out of the human experience and into a perspective where he/she won't have an opportunity to make that mistake again for a really long time.

In other words, that soul is backed up into an incarnation as a life-form without Free Will, probably as a humanoid in another dualistic world, but one without Free Will. However, personally, I like to imagine those souls who behaved like pigs reincarnating as actual pigs. If that's too much of an insult to the pig, they might incarnate into a lower life form. I like to think that the worst offenders might come back as peaceful rocks sitting on a hillside for a few thousand years, and then slowly work their way up from there

When people die who are in this world now, things will be settled just as they've always been. They'll go to the places they need and deserve just as they always have before. However, when the shift happens, those living on the Earth will go to one of two places.

They will either evolve with the Earth, or they will continue as usual on an earth that looks and acts the same as the one they've always known. These people will have been so sure that they were right about the nature of reality that they will actually create that reality as proof. They will create a new soul which they will mistakenly call Earth.

So, the story of unlimited, "Free Will," power in the hands of people who either don't understand it or refuse to believe in it will continue. Their denial of human potential, which is beyond what they can physically see and comprehend, will create by far the greatest miracle any dualistic race has ever accomplished since the dawn of time!

It will launch phase two of Genesis, unbeknownst to those involved but marveled at by everyone else. The illusion of captivity will be renewed and divine Free Will in a dualistic world will have a new beginning.

Beyond that new beginning, NO ONE knows what's going to happen. That's the nature of Free Will. All we can do is watch and see. We might have a better idea though somewhere around the "end of time."

Stay tuned. Film at 11:11—on 12/21/12. Then, by 2014, we all need to be ready to hang on for the ride of our lives!

Our vibrations and the vibrations of
Mother Earth are rising. All we need
to do...is to stay in harmony with
the one thing, which is charge of
EVERYTHING.

In the meantime, the appearance of
things is deceiving. Our understanding
of the world events may get pretty
fuzzy. As magnetism drops, Mother
Nature is helping us ease...out of
our minds and into our hearts.

18

Paint Your Wagon

Where I'm goin I don't know. How I'll get there I ain't certain.
All I know is I am on my way.

These immortal words sung by Lee Marvin in that old movie classic, *Paint Your Wagon*, pretty much sum up the way many of us feel about our evolving lives and the changing world. Just like singing on the big screen was new territory for Lee Marvin, every step we take lately takes us deeper into a world that looks more different every day. Even while the glimmer of this hope brightens, the realities of life for many continue to get more difficult, dangerous, and discouraging.

Political, social, and economic turmoil breaks down our confidence in the systems of career, home and family, and our place in them. Even those few with relative stability in their lives are experiencing a sense of loss and devaluation of their traditional relationship to life. We seem to have little or no control over what's important, and what we physically do each day seems less and less important to many of us.

This can all be seen as an economic and social change. However, our changing perceptions are really the unseen cause behind all of the changes. Our left and right brain are beginning to integrate, causing everything to seem different. This is happening at least in part because of the dropping in the Earth's magnetism. The lessening of magnetism destabilizes the grid which holds our emotional and mental patterns steady and (along with controlled desperation) opens us up to find creative alternatives.

As a result we see things differently. Many look for a higher purpose than the one they see in their current lives. World events feel more discouraging. Many tend to feel depressed and useless as they look for more significant meaning and potential in life.

The increasing *base resonance frequency* of the Earth may also make our joints and head hurt. It makes us fatigued and irritable as our bodies work to catch up with the frequency of the Earth. An inner knowing of the change to come also makes us feel disjointed from our lives and those around us. Suddenly, we aren't too sure about anything! We don't know where we're going, or how we'll get there. We know we're on our way, but we're not sure where we're going so we can't always even be sure it's worth it.

As we push our wagon over the rocky terrain into untraveled territory, we see a whole world of changes. Like changing stations on a television, suddenly the scenes and experiences shift from our old familiar station to one we've never seen before. Actually, the station switched when the new grid was completed in 1989. We've just been trying to tune in ever since. When enough people agree that the picture is clear (which will happen when our vibrations rise a little more), then we'll all make the shift to a new comfort zone and agree on reality again. It's been explained to me that the new world is still in the creation process. They say, "It's not solid yet."

What exactly would make it solid? Are there some 5th dimensional planet builders working overtime on it? Yes and no. We are the planet builders, and **thoughts are the things out of which our new world is being created.**

Mother Earth has put out the intent to evolve to a higher dimension, but (because of her connection to us) she won't go until at least a significant contingent of souls from our current world is in agreement with that vision.

This isn't something we can push. We don't have to try to believe any-thing to which we can't relate. It's all about honesty, and we just need to stay open to the possibilities. Everything is happening in divine order. Our vibrations and the vibrations of Mother Earth are rising. All we need to do to get by as easy as possible AND to assure our place on the evolved Earth is to stay in harmony with the *one thing* which is charge of EVERYTHING.

In the meantime, the appearance of things is deceiving. Our under-standing of the world events may get pretty fuzzy. As magnetism drops, Mother Nature is helping us ease out of our old priorities and into atone-ment—**out of our minds and into our hearts.**

While the magnetism drops, the Earth's *base resonant frequency* rises. This frequency is the electrical discharge pulse of the Earth. You can think of it as a heart beat, but it's more like the fluttering of hummingbird's wings as short, subtle bursts of energy are released many times per second.

In the 1950s, a German scientist by the name of Schumann noticed that these bursts of energy could be observed and measured in the Iono-sphere. Hence, this observable frequency in the Ionosphere has come to be known as the *Schumann resonance frequency*. Lately, this frequency has been observed to be rising.

In the late 1950s, the frequency was around 7.83 hertz. However, recent observations have recorded frequencies between 9 and 11 hertz, which is quite an increase in just fifty years. It's anticipated that this frequency will hit 13, which is the next Fibonacci target after 8.

The natural order of the Universe, such as the way branches grow, etc., which a monk named Fibonacci discovered, goes like this: 1, 1, 2, 3, 5, 8, 13, 21 and so on (just like the sentences of the paragraphs in my Intro-duction, incidentally).

Billy says the Schumann scale, which measures the Earth's vibration in the Ionosphere is a little higher than the actual natural Earth fre-quency. Thin air is a lot lighter than earth, so I guess it makes sense that it would vibrate faster up there. However, it's not a lot faster. The Schul-man scale is still a good tool for measuring the earth's vibration. Science assumes that the frequency, which was first discovered at 7.83, had been constant for probably thousands of years. I suspect that it had actually been resonating at 5 on the true natural frequency scale, and just rose to what Schulman measured as 7.83 in the 1950s.

The frequency at which we currently vibrate is important because Billy has confirmed that we can use this scale as a predictor of the ascension process. When we stabilize at 13 on the natural frequency scale (which is just a little lower than 13 on the Schumann scale) the Evolved Earth on the higher dimension will become solid, and many will begin to ascend to it.

The two worlds will actually share the same space, and the door between them will be open for a while for those who have ascended with the Earth. Those who chose the 3-D path and are insisting on fulfilling their old contracts won't have that option. That was never part of their life contract and simply isn't consistent with it. However, those who evolve with the Earth will be able to go back and forth, and many may want to do this for a variety of reasons. They may want to finish off old business, or help loved ones understand as much as possible and make a new beginning.

However, very few on the new 3D Earth will ever really understand. Also, that door between the worlds will shut when the evolved earth, which greatly accelerates in vibration after it hits 13, finally levels out at 21 on the natural vibration scale (or slightly higher on the Schumann scale). The new 3D earth will remain at 13, the same frequency the original Earth reached at the time of the split. The two Earths will then be totally separate worlds with so much new potential that most everyone will be happy to just move on.

Billy explained in channeling that those who choose to remain on the 3D earth (of their own creation) will feel very uncomfortable. They'll feel like something is wrong. Their bodies will be fighting themselves as the natural inclination to match their frequency to that of the ascending Earth is countered by their Free Will, which has chosen realities that are no longer compatible with the natural things around them

~~~

Like we did at the beginning of time, some of us will turn their back on the one reality, and create something we try to believe is real. After working with that illusion for a while, we then begin the path back to unity awareness again. Sooner or later, we all learn that our feeling of separation from others is simply an illusion brought on by our own will power and a universe that sets up conditions to accommodate our desires.

Those who want to avoid this uncomfortable separation need to paint their wagons with love and trust. If a rickety wooden wagon from the old west is too hard to relate to, imagine a multicolored, flower-decorated, vintage Volkswagen from the 1960s carrying you to the new world. We've matured a lot since those "peace and love" days. Still, we need to "become like children" (flower children?) in order to make the shift as easy as possible.

So paint that Volkswagen, hang your beads on the rear view mirror. Hop in, and drive just as if you knew that thing would keep on running. No fear allowed. The shift is just around the corner. Imagine how disappointed in yourself you'd be if you looked back at this time and realized you blew it when you were SO close!

Each day leading up to this shift brings new opportunities to practice this rite of passage. In that sense, opportunities which test our fear are our friends. Each new experience conquering fear brings us that much closer to our goal of total reliance on the *one thing*. Expect life to bring you face to face with your worst fears. Then drop that fear before it actually happens.

It's no coincidence that these times are hard for everyone right now. The universe is forcing us to choose to pull in our awareness, looking for familiarity and safety, or to trust and embrace the expansion of our horizons. Things all around are conspiring to test our reactions.

If our reactions are compassionate for others and not fearful for ourselves; if we can experience surprises without judgment and feel connected to everyone and Mother Earth, then this connection will pull us right along with the ascension. This practice of balance and feeling love without fear will make us ready for the ride and reward of a lifetime!

When I was first told about the split and how all the animals will be ascending with the Earth, I asked if all we have to do is to be close to nature like the animals in order to tie ourselves to the ascending Earth. I was surprised when Billy said it was more complicated than that. After pondering that for months now, what I've come up with is that it would be that simple if we had a simple nature like the animals. Having Free Will to choose an alliance with the Earth or the completion of our original life contracts, or choosing to not decide, complicates the process. However, for those choosing to ascend, let's use what we know about animals as our goal. How hard can it be to be as good as a dumb animal?

Animals don't anguish mentally when they feel physical pain. They don't plan around fears. They don't worry. They accept life as it is, and they adapt without an existential crisis. Little kids are that way too incidentally. True, it's not as easy for us to be one with nature as it is for animals and little kids. However, trying to be like them in many ways makes achieving this unity with nature a lot easier!

I asked Billy if maybe teenagers might have a difficult time making the shift because of their obsession with their egos. I asked if maybe ADHD kids might have a hard time because of their lack of balance. I asked about a lot of special situations which I thought might make it especially hard for one group or another to ascend with the Earth. In the end, there was only one group that he said would have a hard time. That was the older generation because of their/our fixed ideas of how things are. This brought up another interesting question: "Will there be a lot of kids ascending without their parents?"

To that question I got a resounding "Yes!"

I think about that answer every time my kids talk about adopting when they grow up. All my kids have brought that up, and I'm sure someone on the other side must be planting this thought to help things work out smoothly when there are suddenly lots of parentless kids around.

What this means to the rest of us, who weren't really planning on any more kids but do plan on ascending with the Earth, is that even after we've "made it," we still aren't going to be able to take a vacation from caring. We won't have won a ticket to a world totally without challenges. Expect to have some unexpected responsibilities. We're going to need to continue to use the trust and flexibility that enable us to ascend, and keep right on deferring to the guiding principle of love and compassion.

Trust, flexibility, love, compassion and harmony are all choices that we'll be making more and more as things get more intense between now and the aftermath of the split. I think we can plan on a lot of our long term life plans crashing and burning in the next five years or so. However, even as they go up in smoke, the phoenix rises. As magnetism drops and our brains struggle with our preconceived notions and attachments, the thoughts of our hearts will become increasingly more conscious.

More conscious hearts combined with our rising vibration helps us see through the veil around this world, and brings us more in touch with our higher qualities. Psychic abilities are growing, and the beauty of the new world is sparkling through more all the time for those with an inclination to see it.

Promise yourself and Mother Nature to spend at least a little time each day outside where you'll surrender your priorities to her higher purpose. While you're out there, reexamine your commitments with a focus on your bond to your loved ones and Mother Earth. Let your attention to those things in life that belittle you fall away as you gather yourself around the simple things, which really matter…Feel simple, and simply feel gratitude for the beauty of nature and developing new order.

19

Shifting Awareness

Awareness of this shifting reality rises as the Earth's resonance frequency rises. Our vibrations rise as we're pulled up by the Earth's rising vibrations, and as we respond to the same influences as the Earth, such as gamma rays. Vibrations are rising faster all the time, but so far, it's been a fairly steady rise

After 2013, when planet X flies by, the magnetic poles of the Earth will flip, and then the actual Earth will probably flip on its axis some. This will cause a rush of energy in the earth and its vibration will increase greatly in a short period, just like we might experience a rush of adrenalin during an accident

Our vibration matches the earth's increase, throwing us into "reset mode," as we approach "phase conjugation" (that point at which the wave vibrations come together to manifest a new physical and spiritual reality). When the magnetism drops precipitously and the poles shift, we'll probably experience 20-30 hours in this reset mode as all thought stops except for an awareness of our unity to all things. It's said that this takes place in what we'll experience as a black void. After this, we'll all have a much higher vibration. Yet, that's still not the widely anticipated ascension.

෴

There's confusion because the "phase conjugation" that sends us to a new dimension (either lower or higher) has always come during this period in the void before. However, this time, people have a choice, and it needs to be a peaceful experience. So, after all the physical excitement, there'll be a period to regroup. This is where people either let their consciousness soar with the new natural order Mother Earth has chosen, or discipline themselves to stick to what they know is right, thereby confirming their life contracts in the 3-D world.

During this time, the earth's vibration should stabilize around 13 on the Schumann Resonance scale, and everyone's personal vibration should be resonating at about that same level. Billy says that we'll probably all have our original 12-strand DNA restored by then too, at least on some level. Sometime, shortly after that, the shift goes into full motion and things start to really get interesting. Personally, I feel the shift will finally culminate about a year to a year and a half after planet X flies by.

You'll know the shift is commencing when everything begins to look more luminous. (Those who are not in harmony with the earth will never experience this.) Colors will appear more vibrant. Things will seem to glow and have auras. As the planes overlap, you'll begin to see things from the higher dimension.

You may see fairies and animals that you don't recognize. You may notice that you can communicate with them. Hopefully, you'll notice that they're friendly. Eventually in the newly evolved world, just like the world in which nymphs and fairies live, there won't be carnivores anymore. However, for the time being, you can take comfort in knowing that the consciousness of the carnivorous animals that evolve with the earth will be evolving just like us. So, especially with our enhanced communication with them, there really shouldn't be any reason for fear.

High protein plants will also quickly evolve, and all carnivores will be converting to vegetarianism before too long. This will take place because of the complementary nature of the two suns, the new one being what we call Comet Holmes today. This energy from the two suns will also affect our biorhythms, allowing us to live longer and healthier lives.

The closer we get to the actual shift, the more unusual things will happen. As our vibrations rise into a harmonic that's not compatible with people who insist on their three dimensional reality, those people will appear to suddenly vanish right before your eyes. From their point of view, we'll also suddenly become invisible.

Just before the shift, people may start looking different too. Partly this is in the eye of the beholder, but it's also partly because those evolving with the Earth will begin to manifest their light bodies over their more familiar forms. Noticing small changes in appearance will be increasingly common leading up to the shift. After the ascension, almost everyone evolving with the Earth will eventually be getting a complete makeover. We'll be healthier and appear younger in most cases.

For those who want to be sure not to miss this ride with Mother Earth to a better place, here is a five-step program to help you **shift your awareness so you can be better aware of the shift** and stay in harmony with it:

1. **SPEND AS MUCH TIME AS POSSIBLE OUTSIDE.** Try to relate to all you see in nature and all you know that's below the surface. Declare yourself part of It. When we're inside, our own creations take over our consciousness. These inside involvements and creations may comprise our individual path in life. However, they need to be put in their place if we hope to secure our niche in Nature as she lightens her load in preparation for ascension.

2. **AVOID OPINIONS AND JUDGMENTS.** We all want things to be as easy and comfortable as possible, and we all think we know how that should happen. However, Mother Earth is running this show, and she has her own agenda. Trust the unseen order and know that Mother knows best. Work on detachment from preferences especially from self-indulgent activities. Rest is a priority that Nature understands, but when we're expected to give up our plans, we need to give them up freely, trusting the Earth and the Universe to provide all that's really necessary.

   Also, try to see life from the viewpoint of the family, friends and foes around you. Those who are cemented into one viewpoint won't be prepared to offer the love and understanding to others which a unity consciousness demands. Nor will they be prepared to let go of their known world and accept the coming massive changes.

3. SIMPLIFY. Spend time and attention on those with whom you feel the strongest bonds. Simplify your thoughts about these people –forget their faults and focus on the love. Simplify your activities, spending all the time you can with those you love and doing things which bring you closer to the Earth. Eat simpler. Be simpler.

4. GRATITUDE.

> If the only prayer you said in your whole life
> was, "Thank you," that would suffice.
> – Meister Eckart

Gratitude can make you happy and flexible and, incidentally, help you catch the ascension bus when it comes along. Work on cultivating a feeling of constant gratitude for the infinite blessings of Nature, no matter what is happening in your outer life. Express this gratitude whenever possible, and hold all complaints until you silence extinguishes them.

5. EXPECT TO BE THE PERSON YOU'VE ALWAYS WANTED TO BE. Just as we prepare to give up our personal comforts and preferences, we need to give up all we think we know about our limitations. The whole world is changing, and we ARE changing with it.

Now go back to Number One and review the program. Promise yourself and Mother Nature to spend at least a little time each day outside where you'll surrender your priorities to her higher purpose. While you're out there, reexamine your commitments with a focus on your bond to your loved ones and Mother Earth. Let your attention to those things in life that belittle you fall away as you gather yourself around the simple things which really matter.

Feel gratitude and express thanks in every way you can for your ability to stand in Nature and to stand in your truth. Know that this is who you are as an individual and as part of the ascending Earth. Let love and gratitude fill your thoughts and feelings.

Billy's quick answer for a busy world where dropping magnetism may make remembering even five steps too difficult, was to "Live in the heart chakra," (the heart of the heart) and always "come from a place of love."

What we feel is what we are. Feel love and get to where you feel and know nature. Feel simple, and simply feel gratitude for the beauty of nature and developing new order.

The difference between this shift and all previous ones is that this time we'll either shift consciously to the new dimension or not at all.

20

New Age Stories

Awhile back I saw one of my daughter's friends in a dream. In real life, she's 14, but in the dream she looked like she was about five or six. I've been seeing her that way lately too even though I physically see her 14-year-old body in front of me. This girl has been having serious, possibly life threatening, problems. Yet in the dream, she was totally happy, playing with her friends. I mentioned to my daughter in front of one of her friends that I saw this other girl as a happy five year old in a dream. Her friend confirmed that their mutual friend was totally happy when she was five or six.

A couple weeks later, when this troubled friend was talking about getting away from home when she was old enough, she said this several times during the day: "When I'm five, I'll be free!"

She said she meant to say 18 instead of 5, but she repeated the original statement "by mistake" several times during the day.

It seems clear to me that her "freedom" is going to come when the Earth ascends. At that point, she'll quickly revert to an age when life was more useful for soul. I think the 5th dimensional me is seeing the 5th dimensional her, and that she is realizing on some level that her potential requires regressing to that younger age. I think this is dawning on her now so it'll be easier to accept when the time comes. She'll be herself, but she'll appear as a five year old and regroup her life at that level.

〜〜〜

I also see my wife reverting back to her twenties before her traumas pushed past the point of being useful challenges. Actually, I saw her as a young, beautiful American Indian woman the other day. When I mentioned that to her, she told me about an experience she had right before moving to Montana. She had a vision of an American Indian woman whom she believed was her future self. In this vision, which occurred several times in meditation and dreams, this woman was on top of a mountain and gesturing to a valley below which Danna knew was Montana. The gist of the experience was that she'd be very happy there.

She does seem to be getting happier in the time I've known her, but like my daughter's friend, ascension is really what she needs to realize her vision and get a fresh start. In her case, I see this physical change occurring overnight, sort of like dieing out of the old life without physically dieing. I believe it will simply work that way for some people who are ready for a major change.

Seeing this friend of my daughter in that dream and getting the confirming story about her saying, "When I'm five, I'll be free," made me look for other examples of how physical appearances and ages may change. I saw one woman whose journey in the new world began with a feeling of intense relief. After that, her physical body just reflected this relief in small ways. This went on for quite a while though as she got increasingly beautiful.

I think the point is that soul is going to manifest what's best for our growth. We'll all have a second chance at doing life in the most constructive way possible. If we have major regrets which encompass the last section of our life, that section will be erased, and we'll go back to an age when we felt positive about everything. Generally though, I think most people are up to speed with their lives, and will only experience small, slow adjustments to their physical appearance. I see myself, for instance, about the same age as I am now, but with more energy and hopefully with more hair.

UPDATE: I just got an update to that. They decided to make me about 30. My new life contract has grown, and I'll need to have the enthusiasm and energy of a 30-year-old to do what I need to do. Besides, Danna will be younger than that, so it's a good plan all the way around. There goes my example of a body not changing much. Still, the point is that our body in the new world will perfectly match our purpose. Those with lots to do will appear younger than those who are just supervising and/ or enjoying life.

Those ascending with Mother Earth will also learn quickly to bi-locate. Their first experience with this will be visiting the 3-D Earth while still on the ascended one. Eventually, many will learn to actually project their entire physical bodies to any spot they want around the world.

Our first experience with bi-location will be when many who evolved with the Earth snap back to the other world (which will occupy the same physical space) out of shock from the shift. It won't feel right there, so they'll come back. They may go back and forth several times before getting comfortable enough to settle down on the evolved world.

I'm happy to report that there are a few historical phenomenons that won't be happening this time. In every shift of consciousness since the first intelligent being settled here, a couple things have happened. People go through about three and a half days of darkness and uncon-sciousness in a void where they lose their memories (at least partially) because of the drop in magnetism. If the magnetism is dropped long enough, like it was after the Atlantean accident, all synthetic materi-als lose their electromagnetic based cohesiveness and begin to disin-tegrate. This is all to help people drop their old mindsets and reorient to a new reality.

I asked if the difference between this upcoming time and all the pre-vious times was possibly because all previous shifts were downward. As it turns out, there was one shift that went up in vibrations (at the begin-ning of the Atlantean period), but the people still went through the void in order to reach their new level. **The difference between this shift and all previous ones is that this time we'll either shift consciously to the new dimension or not at all.**

∾∾∾

We'll make a minor jump in consciousness during a short magnet drop, which we'll experience as that dark void I mentioned. However, we'll come out of it fairly quickly to give Free Will one last chance to assert the direction we want our lives to take. This time people will either avoid the shift by creating a new earth and assuming residence just as if nothing had happened, or we'll evolve with the Earth in full awareness.

Billy states that the reason that we aren't going to go through a serious void this time, which causes us to lose our memories or make manmade things disappear, is simply, "because it won't be to your advantage this time."

If anyone experiences three days of darkness, as many are expecting, it will be (according to Billy) "metaphorically." It will be a sort of darkness brought on by the shock of all the changes. The Earth flip will probably cause 25–30 hours of consciousness-resetting darkness, but it won't be anything like the several days of darkness experienced in the past.

Magnetism will drop, but not so far as to make us lose any important memories, and definitely not far enough to make manmade materials disappear. We may get a little loopy, but the more in harmony with the Earth we are going into the magnetic drop, the less we'll notice any unpleasant sensations.

This process of dropping magnetism is a fine-tuning of the mental body we all share and it's for our own benefit. It's part of the divine system administered by Mother Earth, which helps us break the bonds that hold our old thought and emotional patterns in place, and it won't come around for another 13,000 years. So, start taking advantage of it now by letting go of attachments and practicing your loving connection with the Earth. That's probably the most important thing any of us have to do right now.

After the shift, the vibrations of the evolving Earth really start taking off. People will be confused and many from the evolved Earth will travel between the worlds simply trying to find home. Others will go back to the new 3-D earth to try to explain where all the missing people went.

Generally the power of our expectations will dictate what we see. This is something both worlds will have in common. Even after some people vanish from our view because of the power of their Free Will, their homes and cars and all the things we're accustomed to seeing will remain in both worlds.

It's funny that in previous shifts these things just fell apart and disappeared. This time, not only will they remain, but they'll be duplicated so they can remain in both dimensions. It almost seems like a case of planetary cosmic karma. However, it's just nature doing what's best for us, just as it has always done. As people on the 3-D world begin to realize that they can take the empty homes and other possessions left behind for their own use, it will make the sudden disappearance of the people a little easier to accept.

Gradually, people in both worlds will begin to understand what's happened to some degree. The higher the vibration rises on the evolved Earth, the more the door between the worlds will shut. Then, as I mentioned, when the resonance frequency settles at 21 (or a little over 21 on the Schumann scale), that door between the worlds suddenly shuts tightly. This is to protect the unique, self-sustaining integrity of both worlds.

We'll settle into a mass understanding of our new situation and abilities. All shift considerations will be behind us then. People in both worlds will have a much higher consciousness level and much better DNA with which to begin their new lives.

Physical changes are already taking place, and before the major shift, these changes will manifest in a number of ways. One notable occurrence has to do with a green mist. I'm afraid there's not really a personal upside to that phenomenon, but it is necessary for the Earth to move out of the 3-D reality. The sun's energy combined with gamma rays react with the Earth, helping her let go of the lower realities. There's a chemical reaction in this process which releases green gasses that are toxic to physical life.

When you see this stuff or hear that it's coming, go inside, and block any air leaks the best you can. Turn on an air purifier if you have one.

You can also get white paper masks at a hardware store to help you feel safe when you finally venture out.

I don't know the actual chemical reason that this released gas is green, but it makes perfect sense in light of the Hindu traditional representation of the world. They have a color which designates the various planes of existence. These planes also correspond to our chakras.

Green is the color that designates the vibration of the 3-D Earth plane. It's always been representative of the Earth, but it's really the color of the three dimensional reality which we've come to know through the heart of the Earth. It's also the color of the human heart chakra, which is, of course, connected to the heart of Mother Earth.

Incidentally, the color of green has a wavelength of 5000 Angstroms. Remember all that stuff about the number five being the number of man from a few chapters back? Well, quick—look surprised that both the color of our heart chakra and the heart energy of Mother Earth have a wavelength of 5000.

This heart (green) area is responsible for the release of suppressed trauma. It also is the color of all love in motion on Earth. Before Earth ascends, she will have to release much of the green vibration which tends to attach her to three dimensional realities.

Releasing pent up trauma is painful. Sometimes (as in the release of the green gas) it can be downright hazardous to our health. However, rest assured that this purification is coming from a place of love. It's coming from the green heart center of our Mother Earth. Putting up with the fumes is no more than we'd do for any sick member of our family who needs to purge.

Mother Earth will be purging a lot before moving on to her new life. Those who try to hitch their wagon up to the Mother Earth ship will all undergo a consciousness screening, and many disharmonious types will be purged out. This is really a process of harmonizing wavelengths and not as personal as it sounds. Still, the end result will be to lighten the load of those moving on with the Earth since they will all have similar priorities and awareness.

Again, this ascension process is all consciously controlled by our Mother Earth. The situation where many people suddenly go missing is bound to cause concern for those who are left that haven't been told, or can't believe, the plan for both worlds. After this message spreads, people will have a better chance to come to terms with the changes. Yet many, maybe most, never will. Still, as hard as believing is, it's going to be much easier to figure out what's happening after this shift than after any shift in history, because we'll all have our memories intact this time.

That being said, my gut feeling is that the truth about a large section of the population moving to a better place will probably be buried forever. One reason most people won't make the jump with Mother Earth is because they don't believe that it's possible. So after it happens, I'm pretty sure stories will be fabricated to explain things which are consistent with their belief systems. Eventually, even the people who pop back in from the evolved Earth to help for several years will probably be forgotten and memories of them will be dismissed.

However, for those who allow the possibility of ascending to a better place, there won't be a void this time. People will simply slip into the next dimension in full consciousness. The glow around things will get brighter and brighter, and things will look more luminous until we finally emerge into a world with a golden glow around everything. It will have two suns and two moons which reflect the new balance.

It will be a world above duality. Billy says we'll be higher in vibration than the Atlanteans ever were, but not so high as the dolphins are now. Even though they live in our 3-D world, they exist apart from man and in a world all their own. Their consciousness has been a gift to our world, and it will continue to be so on both of the earths after the split.

As I mentioned earlier, another thing both earths will have in common is that the Atlantean machine that caused all the trouble over 13,000 years ago will finally be gone. Our Earth will only be taking natural things which are in harmony with it when it ascends. Not enough people know about that machine to cause it to manifest out of a general expectation on the evolved Earth, and it certainly isn't in harmony with our evolving purpose, so it won't qualify. Also, there aren't enough of the duality destined types who have personal knowledge of it for the machine to manifest in their world either.

After the shift, the people of the new 3-D earth will have just gone through a very uncomfortable time where they felt the separation of their connection with the Earth as she ascended. This discomfort will also have come on the tail end of some traumatic Earth changes and social chaos. Suddenly, they'll notice that many of their friends and loved ones have gone missing. Perhaps they'll show up, but then maybe they'll look different, younger and healthier, and they won't stay. Maybe they'll show up again, and look even more different!

The disappearance of almost half the world's population will be unexplained. People will be putting up posters and asking around, and multiplying the confusion. Everything possible will be done to help ease the trauma of those left on the new 3-D world, but most of the questions will probably never be answered to their satisfaction.

All these changes are in the birthing process already. Even before the outward appearance of the ascending ones changes, there will be some important changes in everyone's bodies and our relationship to reality. As mentioned before, our DNA is changing now, and may be entirely physically restored to the twelve strands (instead of two), which we had before the controlling powers turned us into better slaves at the end of the Atlantean period. If it's not totally physically restored, we will still have better access to it where it exists on the subtler planes. This will restore all of our old qualities and abilities, although those opting to stay in a 3-D world will take much longer to realize these abilities.

On the evolved Earth at least, we'll be able to manifest things much quicker, and many will learn to manifest instantly. We'll live much longer, and be totally healthy. Disease will be a thing of the past. So will crime and poverty.

Instead of laws, we'll have a cooperative consciousness. There won't be any secrets or secret agendas. People will work harmoniously because there won't be any more misunderstandings. Everyone will honor each other with the respect that comes from this understanding. The feelings of insignificance will be gone along with our short sightedness. We'll simply see God and unique beauty in everyone; and everyone will be able to see it in us. There will be managers, but no caste system, and the true authority in charge will be mutually understood by all to be the ruling force of love.

∽∽∽

At the point of the split, the Earth gets a new lease on life. All those who ascend get their 3-D life contracts torn up, and get a chance to make life whatever they want thereafter in a world that's set up to facilitate that. We'll finally be above the downward pull of the hard 3-D realities we've come to know, and find ourselves in a place where our understanding of a gentler reality lightens our step and allows us to breathe easier. Similarly, those on the new 3-D world will get a chance to start over with improved DNA in the world of their choosing.

Without negativity to pull us down, new dimensions of culture, art, creation and exploration will draw us happily upward on the spiraling cycle of enlightenment. We'll be back in tune with the pure positive path where the sky is the limit.

Our experiences with the consequences of separation from the *One Thing* while living on Earth for countless lifetimes will have made us immune to the temptations of ego. The disguises of ego will be transparent, and maintaining balance in this purely positive world will be effortless. After our eventual death, we could always choose to reincarnate in a more difficult and dense world. However, our friends, loved ones, and lives will have a new base. So the need to slip below that new consciousness level won't be nearly as common as it has in the past for those who've earned their way out of the Earth realm. Although life and learning will continue, we really will be home free.

Since the improved DNA will improve communication, better understandings are bound to evolve. A better grasp of our union by all people everywhere would also seem to be a natural outcome.

A Family Reunion

He who experiences the unity of life sees his own Self in all beings, and all beings in his own Self, and looks on every-thing with an impartial eye.
—Gautama Siddharta (Buddha), the founder
of Buddhism, 563-483 BC

Just because someone decides to use his or her Free Will to manifest the appearance of separation doesn't mean that they are in fact separate. God has a claim on us, and we have that same claim on those who will be creating the new 3-D earth. We're all still family.

A long time ago, we were given the freedom to take our attention off our union and create adventures to learn from in the lower worlds. Now, as we return to that unity consciousness, our blessings go out to our bothers and sisters who elect to stay in the third dimension. Mother Earth will also be leaving them with some special blessings.

For the last thirteen and a half millennia, 95% of our brains have been dead weight because ten of our twelve DNA strands were weeded out. Now, as the increase in the Earth's resonance frequency makes unseen changes in our reality, those missing 10 DNA strands are manifesting on subtle levels. By 2012 or 2013 they may be physically manifested for many people.

Yet, the evolutionary magic may not manifest for everyone overnight. These new helixical strands of deoxyribonucleic acid will probably just sit there, just so much more dead weight for most people, until they open up to the new possibilities. Having tools isn't the same thing as using tools.

The reason people will be staying in the 3-D experience is because they have agendas. They have contracts and want to stick with the plan. The new DNA may make telepathic communication much easier, but it'll still be just as easy not to listen. Although the physical tools for understanding others will all be in place, the motivation to do so may not settle in for a while.

However, just as birds are born with the ability to fly but still need to learn how, humans everywhere will discover the advantages of learning to use their new abilities. The difference is that mother birds teach their young how to fly. In the human world, especially before the split, it will be the young who teach their parents.

Those born after 1998, when it became known that the new Earth grid had triggered the upcoming dimensional shift, are particularly good teachers. They came into this world with an awareness of the new plan and a contract for living through the split. They have an innate understanding of those who are using their Free Will to insist on the fulfillment of their 3-D contracts, just as they do for those who are using their Free Will to tear up those contracts, and these children can be a great comfort for all.

Both earths will be getting a fresh start. I've mentioned what it would take to stay in harmony with the evolving Earth. However, just because someone isn't ready to take that ride when the Earth leaves the 3-D realm, doesn't mean love and harmony will totally escape them. A new awareness of unity will be settling in and dawning on everyone, each in their own way, for quite a while.

The Evolved Earth and the new 3-D earth will be sharing the same space. People from the higher dimension will be popping back in regularly to help their 3-D friends and family understand and adjust. Then, once that door shuts, the thousand years of peace, which the Bible promises, is just the beginning for those who make their home on the 3-D earth. It will be a brand new beginning with a lot more enlightenment to work with than we've ever had in the known history of our planet.

There's a really good chance those on the new 3-D earth won't be repeating the same misuses of Free Will that we've all endured for the last 13,000 years or so. Since the improved DNA will improve communication, better understandings are bound to evolve. A better grasp of our union by all people everywhere would also seem to be a natural outcome.

As for my own reunion, it occurred to me that I'm consciously working with five selves. There's that manifestation of me who is the father figure living in the forests of the Ukraine, and that amazing younger woman who lives in India. There's that alternative self who married according to prelife contract and died on schedule. Then there's the man living the academic life, teaching at a college back east in another alternative reality. Two actual physical lives plus two alternative lives as well as the life with which I'm most familiar, makes five lives—all very different, but all very much part of the union of me.

Life for me has gotten to be an exploration of all these different lives as well as ones from my past. This has helped me better understand who this cumulative me is, and what I'm doing. The first obvious observation is that what I'm doing has never been done in a void. All those lives would be empty and eventless if it weren't for the others who've interacted with me in one way or another. Deep loves from the past, present and alternative lives have empowered my understanding of the *One Thing*. Serious conflicts have motivated me to use this understanding of the essence of life to be more than I am.

Seeing how the main evil antagonist I'm aware of from my past became a multi-life lover has been a humbling experience. Seeing how my daughter during several lifetimes (including this one) was a figure-head, whom I viciously fought against during the Bolshevik Revolution, has put a lot of my most passionate efforts in perspective. When I was younger I fought a lot.

I fought against injustices for many thousands of years. I fought for the impossible dream, and it literally drove me crazy! I healed, fought some more and discovered more mistakes.

As we walk through our lives, we can only see so much. Our judgment calls of "good" or "bad," are often wrong. It's been my experience that what we resist usually persists and only results in more humility when we finally surrender to all that we can't really know for sure.

Battles are very real, but enemies are illusive. When we get to really know an enemy, we find a friend. That's when the validity of the whole dualistic world begins to break down. Luckily, we have a new alternative just around the corner. That alternative is all based on our knowledge of unity. The more we get to know, the more our union with the One grows.

> *Life is like a beautiful melody; only the lyrics are messed up.*
> – Hans Christian Anderson

We'll be dealing with the words we've superimposed on Nature's beautiful melody a little longer. There are things my mind tells me I should be doing, but sometimes inactivity seems like the absolutely most appropriate thing to do. As I sit here writing, sipping tea, I feel the beautiful melody of life resounding loudly in my head and heart. When we keep our lyrics silent, the harmony and balance is easy to hear.

To me, teatime has become the fulcrum of life. It's a time when I'm not going to make any serious mistakes, and a time when everything makes the most sense. It's a peaceful break from the teeter-totter of success and disappointment. It's a time of comfort and of dreaming about a better day.

We all *know* that this peace and balance is the one reality. Daily activities can feel completely inconsequential in that light. Even my biggest causes, which compelled me lifetime after lifetime, now seem like the biggest illusions in the world.

Doing what we can to comfort and help those in need, furthers the cause of the One. Pointing fingers and guns at an enemy doesn't. There are no inconsequential acts of compassion. Yet our best reasoned most righteous angry actions could very well be our worst. They separate us from the ability to be satisfied with life, and divide people, thus destroying our awareness of union with them.

Personally, I *see* a new age of harmony for everyone just around the corner. Consciousness is raising and priorities are changing. The light of the realization of unity is dawning on mankind more ever day.

Yet, many are hardening themselves, refusing to see that light. Illusion is the framework of this world and it can be a tremendously powerful tool for those of us who operate in it, pretending to be human. It's an important element in our lives, and I wouldn't take it away from anyone for anything in the world, even if I could. As it is, I *know* I can't. So, the games of life will continue.

I'll continue sipping the cup of whatever life gives me knowing that it doesn't affect the *one* real *thing* at my core one way or the other. Then, when my cup is finally empty, I'll rest in the arms of Mother Earth looking forward to the reunion on the other side. I'll embrace the *one thing* surrounded by its living presence.

I'll *look* on as love dances magically on the stage of life, and *see* its reason for existence in the ever-expanding awareness of the One. I'll walk away from duality and around the corner, go behind that ancient curtain of infinite diversity and stare into the face of God!

Every now and then, I'd wake up
to the true, natural order of things.
Occasionally, I could actually smile
as the grains of sand I tried to
grasp slipped between my fingers.
However, like Edgar Allen, I'd usually
get sad…The good news is there
is a natural order. The bad news is
that most people look for it in all
the wrong places.

22

Natural Order

I stand amid the roar of a surf-tormented shore,
And I hold within my hand grains of the golden sand.
…How they creep through my fingers to the deep
While I weep—while I weep…
Is all that we see or seem but a dream within a dream?
                                                    –Edgar Allen Poe

A s I push aside the curtain, I'm welcomed with open arms. It's tea-time, and it's a much more satisfying brew than I'm used to. It's SO good to finally wake up and find myself home again! After greeting endless groups of friends who seem older than time, I finally ask, "How long have I been gone?"

After, "Well, you weren't really gone," stories start circulating and so do I. Each group remembers a more ancient lifetime than another. Finally, after asking around, the closest we can come to a birth and departure date was over a billion years ago.

After first entering the dualistic worlds on a planet many light years from Earth, I outgrew the dualistic experience only to be sucked back in and stuck again. This happened repeatedly! I would hear the call of love and run to help. I'd think nothing about slipping on another mortal body with its preprogrammed mental and emotional reactions. Nor was

I concerned about living under the morphogenetic field surrounding the planet which shackled my awareness to the consciousness of those on the planet. I'd pretend to be human in a world where everyone was all worked up about pretending to be good or bad, and before I knew it, I was passionately committed to new causes and stuck again.

Every now and then, I'd wake up to the true, natural order of things. Occasionally, I could actually smile as the grains of sand I tried to grasp slipped between my fingers. However, like Edgar Allen, I'd usually be sad; or I'd get really angry!

While living on Earth, my consciousness has normally been buried under reactions programmed into my DNA and surroundings like everyone else. My perspective has been blinded by the commonly accepted truths, which saturate the air. The only clue that there may be suppressed knowledge at odds with conventional wisdom has been my persistent contempt for the harshness of the physical world and my acute awareness of the shallow, selfish motives of others. I've dutifully tried to extinguish these "bad" attitudes my entire life.

Some people want to hear about a better way, but that causes its own confusion. When I or others talk about how beautiful life is and how we are all one, we're talking about life in the dualistic world in the transcendental sense. We're trying to get you to see realities that work in unknowable ways in the world of duality, hiding behind what everyone knows to be true here. We're trying to activate your memory of using a higher knowledge on a higher plane.

Those same principles work in the physical world, just slower. They are essential to working our way out of here. Yet we have to rise above the dream of duality in order to use those principles. The vision of using higher principles actually helps us rise in vibration enough so we can actually use them.

Meanwhile, the common perceptions that have permeated the Earth grid of consciousness continue to dampen all of our attempts to really know those higher, more real truths. Yet, as we struggle to see more clearly, others are doing the same, and the grid is reflecting the new awareness, making it easier for all.

Many want to deny the constraints of circumstances, DNA and Earth grid. They say, "Nothing interferes with your enlightenment except you!" That denial, i.e. illusion, is a very functional approach too. It's simple and removes any excuses from our doing our best. According to Hunt's HH Principle (see the entry under a similar name in Chapter 8 for details on that), our denial of those realities is very likely responsible for many of the positive changes in our circumstances, DNA and even our grid.

Yet, denial of reality leaves us vulnerable to emotional reactions when the denied reality occasionally rears its ugly head and brings defeat, leaving us with no explanation. That's why I've always thought the best approach is to *look* at life as honestly as possible and recognize the challenges as well as the possibilities; to *see* the inconvenient realities, but really focus on the ones that can help us—such as our ability to create reality by seeing it first and holding tightly onto that vision.

The mystic can walk anywhere in any world carrying the *One* essential *Thing* with him, and see the natural order in whatever is going on around her. The good news is there is a natural order. The bad news is that most people look for it in all the wrong places. Whenever we're sifting through our life trying to separate the good from the bad, we're looking through dualistic eyes for realities that never really break down well that way.

It's all so clear as I sit at home fully aware of the loved ones who surround me who've played different roles in my many incarnations. I'd like to think that I'll never leave again or ever sacrifice any consciousness again in order to try to help someone who's in a dark space. Yet, the only resolution I'm totally comfortable with is to pledge to do whatever I do for the sake of love. It's no sacrifice! Love is the womb out of which all good things bloom no matter how bad they may look while they're unfolding.

No matter what dreams we're pursuing, there's always a greater purpose under the surface of things. Whether we feel the joy of success or the agony of defeat, there's always a subtle success growing unnoticed. It's the *one* little *thing* that everyone usually forgets.

Our attempts to right the unrightable wrongs make our love grow. Our anguish makes our love grow. Seeing our plight, others open their hearts to us, and love grows again. Then, when life shows us its lighter side, our love and gratitude make the one love we all share grow even more.

Illusion is a big part of that system which powers and permeates the physical worlds. Dreams are essential, and that won't change when our Mother Earth ascends into the next dimension. The daily realities will be gentler in the evolved world than the dualistic one, but illusion and playing games for which we don't really know the rules will still be equally important in both worlds.

Some of us will pursue more impossible dreams than others. Still, we all play our games and run in our own little circles. Whatever the results, our hearts reach out with hope and love and thus serve the one purpose of the one Source. Regardless of success or failure, or the chaos and craziness we endure, our reactions all serve our unacknowledged mission to learn about love and make it grow.

We all have to *look*, and *see* as clearly as we can. However, hope for success in this crazy house of mirrors isn't dependant on attainment of our goals or even on understanding the ways of the world. Perhaps you've been very successful and feel you have the human condition all figured out. Yet, if you ever catch a little illusion getting mixed up with what you hold as absolute truth just know that it's a valid and powerful part of the divinely ordained system. If your illusion is happy, consider yourself tremendously blessed.

So…

Take this kiss upon the brow!
And in parting from you now,
Thus much let me avow:
You are not wrong, who deem that my
  days have been a dream;
Yet if hope has flown away in a night or in a day,
In a vision or in none, Is it…gone?
All that we see or seem
Is but a dream within a dream."
— Edgar Allen Poe

...it IS possible to know what we need to know if we just believe in that possibility, live as if we have everything we need, and listen expectantly to the guides all around us.

...Love is the tipping point between the human path and the path of our ultimate potential...Our trials may be almost overwhelming, but the dream of Love is infinite.

Epilogue
"A Dream within a Dream"

The dream is the small hidden door in the deepest and most intimate sanctum of the soul, which opens to that primeval cosmic night that was soul long before there was conscious ego and will be soul far beyond what a conscious ego could ever reach.

—Carl Gustav Jung

During the writing of this book, I ventured through many hidden doors and intimate sanctums of my soul. I questioned myself, and I challenged the order of life. Questions led to more questions and carried me deep into the cosmic night, the complete discovery of which, as Jung points out, is totally beyond any conscious ego. Still, I was able to explore some of my experiences in that "dream within a dream" we know as life, and a divine order revealed itself.

After reviewing every concept, issue and answer in this book, as I did many times, it's tempting to lay out that divine order in detail as I see it. However, if we look too closely at the conquests of the mind, we cast a shadow of limitation on that infinite "intimate sanctum of the soul." Those concepts need room to grow and mystery to feed upon. So, I'll just let my creation/my baby stand on her own to be seen by readers in their own way so that, with their help, she can mature and grow without a doting parent critiquing her every move.

However, before I let her walk out the door into the big, wide world, I'd just like to make a small coming-out announcement about who I think she is and what she stands for. Telling you what I see as the "moral of the story" may seem a bit corny and antiquated, but that ancient tradition does serve a purpose. Besides, it gives me one more chance to give you another happy ending, and I LOVE happy endings!"

Ever since I discovered that my daughter, Veda, has a conscious connection to someone who can give her any answers she wants, it's been tempting to ask her questions about my life. However, each time I start, my silent guides make themselves known by flooding my consciousness with waves of their disappointment in me. If I actually go through with my question, which I did as an experiment a few times, those waves practically drown me until I get the point.

I knew I should be a parental figure who didn't need her in that way. Still, I really wanted those answers. Gradually, I began to picture myself as I should be—strong and confident in the Universe... Still, that was just an image, which I had a hard time getting my skin around.

However, during the course of writing this book, that image began to fit better and better. When I'd walk away from a question with confidence in the Universe and in my ability to know what I needed, I found that the answer was just laying there for me when I returned. Slowly, over the last year or so, trust in the unseen has grown so it's actually stronger than faith in what I physically see or think.

So, the moral of the story is that it IS possible to *know* what we need to know if we just believe in that possibility, live as if we have everything we need, and listen expectantly to the guides all around us.

The last thing I just have to say, after putting many lifetimes in perspective and being awakened to this realization by the pain and disappointment of this lifetime, is that **Love is the great purifier!**

Life gives us things to purify. Then, as John Lennon put it, "Love is the answer." Love is the *one thing* which makes all the magic in the universe work.

It's been proven to change the structure of water. It makes plants grow better. Billy says that blessing our food makes it better for us. I discussed how Mantak Chia explains the love principle in terms of the "smile technique" for healing the body.

Drunvalo Melchizedek blessed the world by sharing his merkaba meditation. Yet the focus and breaths his instructors teach are impotent without love in the practitioner to power them. The degree to which that meditation, or any meditation, works depends on the amount of love we put into it.

Love is the tipping point between the human path and the path of our ultimate potential. It's the attraction that holds the world and universe together, and it's the force that holds us together when life seems to pull us apart. Our trials may be almost overwhelming, but the dream of Love is infinite.

We've matched our power against it for millennia. We've imagined ourselves cut off from the *one thing*, and our attempt to create something separate has been pathetic. Now it's time to wake up from that nightmare and realize the dream of the new world.

I'm supposed to tell you that our ascension is all dependent on a significant amount of people coming into better harmony with their loving, trusting nature and, in a word, the *One*. Earth will wait until enough people have made that leap in consciousness. Then, only those who have come into that harmony will ascend with her. Despite the present world turmoil and the ever-present personal chaos, we each need to wake up to peace within ourselves before the new day can dawn.

Seeing how things work can help us believe in the magic. Yet understanding isn't a requirement for *knowing*. Knowledge is the quiet, still, reassuring voice we hear once we tune out the conflict and chaos around us.

Knowing is the sense we learn while we dream in the *intimate sanctum of the soul*.

It's the omnipresence and omnipotence we breathe while we dream. It's the throne we learn to recognize as our own.

〜〜〜

Many renowned scholars say it's not possible to really know anything for certain in this physical world. They make a good point because of what they *know* about this world, which misses most people who take things at face value. We *look* and react. We think we might *see* sometimes. However, anyone who *knows* will tell you that *knowing* just isn't possible in this world.

Yet, the veils are thinning between what soul knows and what our earthly vehicles see. I feel my connection to nature, life, and the ever-pervading loving universe more every day. Seeing this connection, *I know* more about myself and life all the time.

I now know that despite it all, life has a hidden purpose and order. *I know* that life can be absolutely magical as the unseen hand moves in mysterious ways. *I know* I'm protected and guided, and *I KNOW* that I need to remember that, no matter what I think I see sometimes.

The knowledge of the *One Thing* can be more real than any thing we can physically touch. Yet it begins with just a dream. This dream is the magic that starts as a whispering breeze and grows into a tornado, which is carrying us to a whole new world.

Faith in our best dreams and the power of the *One Thing* causes the layers of illusion to gradually peel away, and that leads to a deep satisfaction. In fact, they're telling me right now that it "leads **inexorably** to the knowledge that unravels the mysteries of the soul." That sure sounds like we can't lose, and that is the happiest ending I could ever imagine!

The Story behind *Looking, Seeing And Knowing*

When I was seventeen, I wrote a novel during a high school independent study class which earned me an "A" in the course, but which was written off by a professional critic as having "fatal flaws" even after several entire rewrites. One desperate day, I asked Spirit if I'd ever have anything published. Suddenly, I found myself in library which would dwarf the largest library I've ever physically seen. I went through the stacks until I found a little book with my name on it. It was entitled, *Looking, Seeing and Knowing*.

Not only did I feel totally incapable of writing what I sensed was in that book, but I couldn't imagine myself ever being the person who wrote it. Now I understand why. That person who was me in my earlier life was contracted to follow a path where he left this world a few years ago.

I kept living physically, but after that point, my perspective on life became a lot clearer. I think it probably got almost as clear as if I had gone to the other side like I was supposed to.

I look back at the person I was when I first went to that library on the astral plane, and it's as hard for me to relate to him as it was then for him to relate to me. I AM a new person, and I know when it happened. I was 52, and I'd just finished my first draft of my first book, *The BIG Fake-out*. That was my lifeline as I retraced my life in its pages in an attempt to decipher a life that felt all wrong.

That's when I met my wife, Danna, who channeled a mutual member of our immediate soul family. He began telling me things I couldn't quite understand. This led me to ask about EVERYTHING on the inner. Gradually, answers flowed easier and I grew closer to my own guides.

They'd help me get the concepts right, and kept disturbing me until my presentation of them was at least close enough. I was blessed with a second chance at a better life and so was *The Ancient Secret of the BIG Fake-out,* which was rewritten and retitled *The Big Fake-out, the illusion of limits.*

These answers also finally made sense out of that vision I had decades ago about finding a book in the astral library with my name on it. Suddenly, I realized why I couldn't imagine ever being the person who wrote that book. I never got the material for it until after my contracted life was complete!

Yet I saw it—a dream of a book I was to write in a reality I probably wouldn't ever enter. It was simply "a dream within a dream," and there was nothing to get me from there to here—nothing except the *One Thing.*

Appendix

Continued from Chapter 9, A Live Experiment

July 27, 2007, Continued

Currently, I have two manuscripts with an agent, but nothing has been published so my only source of income is my little home business, which has been declining precipitously for about three years. This year's income has been the worst since I started the business, so I decided to branch out.

Some of my best times with my family were playing poker, so I looked into selling unique poker sets. I risked way more than I could afford to lose on a hope and a prayer. I ran an ad, but was planning on holding off on buying any inventory until I saw how that ad panned out.

Before it even ran, I had a channeling session in which Billy volunteered that my poker ad would do well. I didn't ask him, but since he told me that, I felt compelled to make the most out of this business. I created a special poker chip set for my target audience. I made up some custom chips and brought in what felt like a minimum amount of inventory to cover the various options I was offering. I also obligated myself to a much more expensive ad when the sales rep called back.

The first ad came out about two months ago. To date, it's resulted in lots of leads but no sales. Still, Billy had said that this project would be successful, so when the sales rep called back again, I obligated myself to another huge ad I couldn't afford, and then another one. They were great deals each time, and the last one was placed on the understanding that they would consolidate my bills so I wouldn't have to pay anything for three months. Then, I'd just have to pay $500 per month, which made my approximately $15,000 bill almost manageable. Also, he said he'd make me up a brochure to help get sales, and that he and others there would make sales calls for me. That's four very expensive ads plus inventory, plus a couple months of almost fulltime work, and no sales yet.

JULY 5, 2007, THE PROBLEM BUILDS: On July 3rd, my sales rep informed me that I needed to pay $2,200 right now, and that my brochures (and entire campaign) would be on hold until I did. I reminded him of the deal he had agreed to where I wouldn't pay him anything for a couple more months. I offered to let him off the hook for my brochures. I said I could produce them elsewhere if he'll just give me the artwork. No go. He was holding firm. He absolutely had to have a payment which he had agreed only a few weeks ago that he wouldn't have to have.

He reneged on the deal. Still, I would pay him if I could. I just took out a $10,000 loan a month ago to get me out of trouble from my declining business, and it's all gone. I looked at my checking balance today: $2300 in the negative. I have $1000 overdraft protection, but I clearly can't write another check for $2200. Yet if I don't, all the time and money I've put into this new venture is down the drain, and this investment which was supposed to save me, could end up to be the nails in my coffin. Bottom line: despite my faith in the universe, I'm shook! I'm worried to the point that I can hardly breathe at times.

Something else happened today that added to that mood, too. I saw a doctor who was worried by three moles he saw. When I didn't appear worried, he helped me see his perspective by saying, "Melanoma can kill you as fast as a bullet."

"Thanks Doc. I'll call you."

HYPOTHESIS #1: LIFE IS TURNING TO CRAP AGAIN. I'm sorry, but as anyone who's been through times where things just keep going from bad to worse to the point where you really wish you were dead can attest to, that is the first hypothesis that comes to mind when something bad happens again. Now, I understand that it's not because the Universe is trying to prepare me to fulfill the contract of leaving the world early anymore, but maybe it's because of the downward momentum of my life that accrued while I was being prepared to leave this world. Perhaps my gut attitudes, which hide under my positive affirmations, are still based on this downward momentum. Perhaps it's old karma. Or perhaps there are new lessons in the works. The particular reason should pan out by the end of this experience. Still, whatever the reason, all the possibilities along this line of thinking still add up to a life turning to crap again.

HYPOTHESIS #2: THIS IS JUST THE OPPORTUNITY I NEED to show myself that with some positive energy and creative thinking, I can turn bad situations into good ones. Also, it's an opportunity to practice standing firm in the face of danger, holding onto a positive resolve and not giving into fear.

HYPOTHESIS #3: SHIT HAPPENS, and that's all there is to it. I remember the Buddhist principal of *"Sancho Shima."* It literally means *"three obstacles and four devils."* The principle recognizes the balance of positive and negative and warns of negative experiences whenever anything powerfully positive is occurring. In other words, especially when things are looking up, shit happens.

I expect that I'll conclude that #3 is valid no matter what else I decide. However, I'm going to chronicle what happens financially or in any way which seems related to this experiment, live as it happens.

The first thing I have to report is just a dumb little thing that may mean nothing. Still, in my intense state, it felt significant.

I was trying to cram more under the bathroom sink than I really should when it occurred to me to turn on the hot water, which I had turned off months ago when the hot water leak had become a strong stream which I couldn't shut off any other way. The fix for this modern faucet involved replacement, which I figured I couldn't afford, so I just turned off the hot water a couple months ago.

Anyway, when I turned on the hot water there wasn't so much as a drip. I don't know much about plumbing, and there could be a logical reason for this. However, when I was looking for some positive sign that hypothesis #1 wasn't correct, this felt like a message from God!

This evening, I formulated a plan with my better half. I still have just enough on one of my credit cards to give this blood sucking, lying vendor what he wants. If I haven't heard anything from any of the managers by 11 A.M. their time tomorrow, I'll pay the $2200 with my Visa.

We confirmed with each other that life and prospects are still good. Personally, I resolved to really test this positive energy stuff. In my own mind, it would be better to die with inner strength and resolve than to live with the kind of worry which almost killed me in the past.

July 6, 2007, The Saga Continues (with a hug): The first email I read today was from an old friend who was sending everyone he knew a hug today. He said that in 52 years as a healer, he'd probably hugged about 200,000 people. Today he was sending us all a virtual one. That helped me start the day off right.

11 A.M.: no emails from managers seeing the light, so I paid what they wanted and, ignoring the understated conflict, I talked positively with my sales rep about the campaign—so I can get as much cooperative work out of him as possible before I break the news to him that I don't do business with people who don't honor their deals. I hope to stretch that cooperative phase out at least three or four months.

Also today, I did call that doctor back to take care of that little medical issue. I don't want to have gotten this far just to have some little thing trip me up and put me down.

July 22, 2007, Lessons on Conflict: My twelve year old daughter was looking for comfort from some distressing situations one evening when an old (non-physical) friend from a previous life came to her.

"Hello Babe!"

That's how he always greets her. He thinks it's really funny that's she's a cute little girl after the lifetime they shared as mountain men in 18th Century America.

Sweeping his arm broadly across their vision of the Universe, he simply said, "It's all just a front. It's a cover-up. Nothing you see is real."

When she told me about this and asked what it meant, I wasn't sure what to say. I'd given her the talk about the many dimensions of existence and relative realities many times. So I just said, "Whenever something upsets you, just remember it's not real. Just keep telling yourself that."

I ran this by Billie a week later to see if he had anything else to add to that. This is what he said: "You can't be in a place of fear. The only thing that's real is love. Conflict is a fear-based illusion. We create them in order to learn."

So if our conflicts really are under our control, then we don't have anything to be afraid of. This felt like a fresh, living example of the stuff I'm known for decades. Still Earl's humor and looking at life's challenges through my little girl's eyes has helped me remember that everything we're afraid we know about the world is wrong!

There's just a universe of potential waiting out there for us to decide how we're going to relate to it. With this thought it's easier to reinforce my joyful focus on the abundance, which lets me carry on my life's mission unhindered. After visualizing a nurturing bubble of protective love around each of my kids, my daily prayer is a happy confirmation and gratitude for the order and success in my own life.

July 25, 2007, One Problem Solved: "The lord giveth and the lord taketh away."

A couple days ago, God gave me another challenge for my peace of mind. I'd been hearing a clunking sound in the rear end of my car whenever I changed gears, and decided I'd better get it checked out. After checking it out, the mechanic said, "You have big problems."

That's exactly what I didn't want to hear—for practical reasons and for some existential ones. I was really hoping to prove that hypothesis #1 wasn't correct.

He gave me a price, and I told him I'd have to wait. I was wondering how I'd make my next mortgage payment when I had come in there, and now I had this! Then on the way out the door, God gave me another challenge for my peace of mind when the mechanic said, "Don't wait too long. It could go out any time."

A day later I went to different mechanic for another quote. He took one look at it and told me that my differential went out because on an all-wheel drive vehicle, all the tires need to be the same size and mine weren't. Armed with this information I went over to the shop that had sold me the tires hoping that they'd take some responsibility for my problem.

The owner agreed to put two new tires on that would match two of the old ones. I was expecting some sort of prorated exchange, but it soon became clear that it was going to be a straight swap. Then we talked about the differential. He told me to get quotes, and I still wasn't sure what exactly he had in mind. Here again, I figured that there would be some sort of prorated calculation for taking off my differential, which had over 175,000 miles on it, and putting on a good one. However, today when I turned in my quotes, he told me he would be taking care of the entire thing, labor and all! I got new tires in trade for my old ones and a new/used differential in trade for my extremely used and broken one—free!

The monstrous problem was suddenly removed from my life. It happened so quickly and so completely that it felt like a message from God: "Life is good, and your life is definitely NOT turning to crap."

July 27, 2007, And Still the Challenges Mount: It's hard to believe that the blessing above happened a couple days ago already. I've been trying to hold onto it as if it just happened so I could continue to feed on its nurturing implications. Still, life goes on. The medical issue at the beginning of this journal, culminated yesterday with a doctor carving off a piece of my flesh about the size of a quarter. Ever since then, that's been a constant reminder of the test to focus on healing rather than on painful problems.

For quite some time, I've been hoping to solve my biggest problem in one fell swoop with a real estate sale. However, the long awaited day of my financial salvation finally came and went. The offer of one third my asking price left me with only a shocking renewal of that same choice: to focus on hope and healing or the pain of the problem. Actually, that challenge has been taken up a notch with the fairly complete destruction of one of my biggest hopes.

When I'd first talked to a realtor and surveyor about subdividing a section of my little (less than 6 acre) plot, prices had been skyrocketing. However, in the last year and a half, while I was investing in subdivision red tape, that rocket seems to have landed. When I finally met with my neighbor as a potential buyer yesterday, he offered less than my costs of subdividing the land (after the road improvements I still have to make). If you throw in my original costs of the land, I lose significantly! If you throw in the fact that I was counting on this to bail me out of my financial nose dive, you can begin to understand the challenge to my positive attitude this little surprise presents.

I didn't let fear get a hold. I immediately went down to a realtor and officially listed the property. They confirmed the reality of the new "softness" of the market, but also gave me hope of making a much better sale than that offer represented.

Tonight, as I look out into the friendly forest, I have to smile at the invisible beings who I know are looking back at me, safely hidden from the physical demands of our human world. A prayer for unity with the beauty and bounty of nature all around me fills the spot in my heart where the desire for escape used to reside. The difference between looking for comfort in the experience of divine order and looking for comfort by escaping to where divine order is more obvious (in the after life) feels like a really small distinction. However, it is the difference between life and death.

It occurs to me that each day we make that choice in little ways. Being optimistic and having a positive attitude is choosing life. Facing the obvious negative with a reasonable amount of fear and dread is to choose death. Of course we don't think of it that way. Still, everyday in little ways, dread brings us ever closer to dead. So, what's more reasonable—rational fearful reactions, or seeing the world through the creative flowers of fantasy?

I really believe that there's a happy reality which usually hides just outside the reach of our rational minds. Tonight, I just want to lose myself in the loving, nurturing nature of all the wildlife around me. I feel its love. I know that in reality, that's all there is! From there, it's a small step to believing in my harmony with health and happiness.

I like to think I have an idea of what life may have in store for me, but health and wealth are illusive goals. As I prepared to meet this day and the potential buyer, I knew attachment to my hopes and expectations was dangerous. I thought I had let go of them. However, since I didn't have a backup plan, I was still vulnerable.

I suppose I should thank the Universe for pointing that out to me. Perhaps now, I can work more freely at increasing my trust in the everpervasive mystic laws. Coming into harmony with that trust is really the only dependable backup plan.

JULY 29, 2007, COUNTING MY BLESSINGS: Now that I've emerged back into the world, I realize that I'd slipped into a serious retreat mode for the last couple of days. After that medical procedure and after that financial disappointment, I needed healing. I didn't eat or sleep regularly, but I did write a lot and I contemplated my blessings constantly.

It was a strange space without fear. I felt a desperate devotion to what I feel my mission is, and as long as I stayed busy, fear was held at bay. I've discovered many times now that powerful emotion is what seems to make the magic work. It's worked over and over. I'll get right to the give-up point when suddenly things totally change.

It's definitely a blessing and a gift, but I think it may also have something to do with the emotional, harmonizing power put into the prayer. The trick is to turn desperation into a constructive tool. So, added onto the list of what I'm grateful for is this blessing of another chance to practice this art.

Another blessing I count right up there at the top of my list is living with a channeler. I've always wished I had something original to write about, and I've always thought it would be cool if I could just ask about stories and principles and get the answers channeled to me. Today we had a session in which I asked an exceptionally long list of difficult questions.

There were long silences as Billy looked back through history or forward in time to see my answers. I was delighted to get a clear picture even though some of the information contradicted other things I've read. I was satisfied that I had gotten the definitive answers when Billy said: "...But don't take my word for it. Research it on your own." He suggested reading Zecharia Sitchen, for instance, to help me get at some of the ancient history, and he said to ask my own guides in order to get the fine points straight.

I always listen to my helpers when I write, but I've also always thought of the channeled answers as the final word. I'll still double check information I get on my own through channeling to make sure there isn't any problem with it. However, his advice that my own guides are my highest authority was enlightening.

Of course it's true, but I never focused on it. Now that I do, it increases my awareness of my presence here on Earth. It helps me realize who I am, what I'm doing, and the validity of my existence at a time when that's all fairly new to me. I really am starting over, and the realization of that fact is the biggest blessing of all!

July 30, 2007, Darkest Before the Dawn? After I got that really low offer for my property, I did more homework and narrowed the comparable lots (sold and listed) down to six, which I thought the buyer would agree were indeed very similar. The average was well over twice what he was offering. I went to his office with this info along with a note detailing what the property was obviously worth and how'd I'd make him a deal by coming down a bunch from that average cost. Since he wasn't in, I left that info for him.

I had also listed the property, but the improvements I need to make to fulfill the subdivision requirements would cost over $25,000. That's why I keep seeing my neighbor and the possibility of a boarder adjustment (which would get around subdividing) as my best possibility. I try not to get attached to ideas, but my three credit cards are all over their limits, the bank account is overdrawn up to the limit of my "overdraw protection," and the bills just keep coming in much faster than the income. So, when I think about it, which I try not to do, I start to feel a little desperate and expect an answer right away, and this is the only one I can even remotely imagine working right now.

I really feel trusting most of the time. I'm looking for an answer to make a happy ending to my story. However, reality keeps rearing its ugly head, and testing my resolve. Each time, the impact hits me harder. When my neighbor reviewed my new evidence of the property's worth, he called me up and simply reiterated what he felt it was worth to him.

I hung up the phone with the satisfaction that I had done my job in helping my neighbor make the best informed decision possible. Then my heart dropped. What was I supposed to do now?

I went for a walk with my wife. After we assured each other that everything was going to be fine, there was silence for quite a while. As I walked looking at the forest for assurance, I contemplated that saying: "May we be worthy of our challenges."

I'm not sure how worthy I am exactly, but I do still expect a happy ending to my story. To the casual reader this may all just sound like whining. However, in my own little life, I feel the climax building and can only wonder what could possibly happen to resolve the situation, which looks pretty impossible right now.

Still, my job is to stay positive. Thank God for vegetables from the garden. I'm not sure what we'd be eating if it weren't for the garden. Despite life's little dramas, home grown roasted carrots, onions, potatoes and zucchini would be worth coming to Earth for all by themselves.

AUGUST 2, 2007, MORNING MUSINGS: It just occurred to me that although I get worried sometimes about prospects not panning out as I expected, mainly I'm just sitting back wondering what the bigger picture is that I'm not seeing. I'm wondering about what the Universe has in store for me which closing these doors might entail. That's quite a difference from just a few short years back when similar disappointments made me feel that the natural order of things was preparing to recycle or compost me.

Actually, I believe now that it was. At the time, I was hoping it was just my bad attitude. Back then, during the brief times when I wasn't feeling sorry for myself, I was really angry!

Anyway, the way I see things has really turned around. I wonder if the art made by starving artists really benefits from the starving of the artist. I am practicing my art of writing a lot these days. There's not much business going on to interfere with it.

I dream about being published and well accepted, but then if I were a popular writer, I wouldn't have as much time to write. I guess everything's okay. I'd ask in channeling but the answer I always get is "everything is going to be fine." I have to ask really specific questions to get more than that, and then I really don't get anything that sounds like a definitive answer.

"Everything is going to be fine:" Isn't that what you'd tell anyone no matter how bad things look?

On the other hand, when I started this public journal, it was with the idea of illustrating that I'm not leading a privileged life. Okay, Universe: mission accomplished. Now let's get on with the happy ending!

AUGUST 7, 2007, HHHP (HUNT'S HAPPY HORSESHIT PRINCIPLE): I've been wondering about what Billy said a while back: "If you pull too hard at the loose strings, the whole thing unravels."

It came up when we were talking about what if I had taken other paths. I got my personal answers from my own guides after Billy's warning, without any mishap. However, today, as my desperation about personal issues formed questions, Billy's comment came back to me.

Basically, today I'm beginning to wonder if the failure in my business, and the utter failure in the business I went out on a limb to start to replace my failing business, AND the sudden drop in real estate prices to half of what it was just six months ago, which might otherwise have bailed me out, may all be conspiring to test my reactions. I was okay with that thought for a while, but lately I've been beginning to wonder how many more sacrifices are going to be expected by the god of fear (metaphorically speaking) before he's done with me.

I find I can operate with high energy if I don't think about it too much. I actually expect that everything will be okay if I just don't put any energy into the negative possibilities. That brings us back to what Billy said about not pulling too hard at the loose strings.

I really want to know what's going on, and I feel compelled to pull on all the loose strings I can find! It's a personal flaw. That's what I do! However, in this case, it's probably better right now NOT to know what's really going on.

God, or the universe, protects the dumb. Not knowing what's happening may be the only way to actually get through it. If we knew what we were really up against, fear would take over and put holes in our boat of benefits, which our minds build with our positive thoughts.

So, believing all is well (and Happy Horse 'it like that) helps make it so. Our creative energy and expectations are what create the fabric of our worlds more than any objective reality. Actually, my "objective" opinion on Objective Reality at this point is that, if it involves humans, (rather than something we can observe outside our realm of influence), it's a myth. We affect absolutely everything we touch or even think about, individually and as a group. Reality, as it relates to us, is a dynamic moving force, which moves according to "the ultimate of our expectations." (A Tibetan monk by the name of Rebazar told me that "on the inner" when I was just a kid about 12.)

Our conscious expectations seem to actually have counterproductive results sometimes as our higher self demonstrates what's real to us and what's really important. Even so, reality is still affected by our affirmations, our energy…, and by our ignorance. **Ignorance is the grease which**

keeps the machine of the whole physical world running smoothly. It's definitely a weird world.

AUGUST 8, 2007, THE MYSTIC'S APPRENTICE: I learned about pulling events, things and people into harmony with what the heart of heart wants from Pythagoras (See *The Don Q Point of View*, for that story). Hundreds of years (several lifetimes) later, I forgot Pythagoras's stern warning against the use of this magic for personal gain, and I abused the power with great success. I've been in a strict rehab ever since.

I did all sorts of penance in the lifetimes that followed. I suppose it could be wisdom that makes me resist using it now. However, it's probably more of a conditioned response thing, like shocking a rat every time it goes down the wrong path.

Anyway, I've had an aversion to innocent talk about "positive thinking," or prayers for what we want all my life. However, I've been examining all that lately, because if ever there were a time to "pull a rabbit out of a hat" this would be it!

I've been thinking a lot lately about that life I lived as evil magician. I can feel his power and confidence. Yet, when I try to understand how he really did it, I feel myself starting to go down a log dark tunnel, which I know better than to enter.

Part of me wants to be his apprentice, but I've also learned an appreciation for the unknowable will of the universe. When you soften up on acceptance of results, all of a sudden you move from magic to mysticism in which the universe uses you as much as you use it. The focus is divine unity, rather than a psychic tool to help you leverage physical results. I know what I want, but I can never really know what's in the best interest of the whole.

When I contemplate that magician, I'd like to keep his confidence, but lose his practice of manipulating Nature. Those strings need to be pulled by someone in a higher, more detached state of consciousness—for lack of a better word, God.

The difference between the magician and the mystic is that the mystic doesn't know what particular short-term outcomes to expect. He just gracefully moves through his day, staying in touch with his guidance as much as possible, and doing his jobs to the best of his ability. He expects the best possible result from his focus on the One. Yet, because it's impossible to know the mind of God, he never knows for sure what that result might look like. May I be worthy of this path of blissful ignorance.

AUGUST 9, 2007, HOLDING THINGS TOGETHER: Last night I dreamt I was on a giant airline flying miles above the earth. I wasn't IN the plane: I was ON the tail section, holding one of the wings on. Somehow, there was a cargo hold in front of me with 25 gallon barrels rolling around and falling out whenever the plane banked and turned. At those times, I'd have to let go of the wing with one hand and try to keep the barrels from falling on me or falling out with the other.

I lost a few, but I saved a lot too. Somehow, there was someone just sort of floating alongside with encouragement. "Ooo, that was close…. Good job! You saved those!" He'd say things like that, which helped some, but it was still all up to me.

I don't' remember landing. But I did finally wake up. One thing I just noticed: It's interesting how yesterday I was thinking about "pulling on loose strings" and wondering how things fall apart; and then last night I dreamt about the extreme danger of holding things together.

I'm not sure what the message is. If it were anyone else, I'd say "Try not to ask too many questions so you don't find yourself miles above the world in mortal danger with an impossible task!"

However, this is me we're talking about. I don't think I can really do anything different except to hold on even tighter to the One Thing and plan on not being blown away by fear. God help me.

AUGUST 9, 2007, TIME TO WAKE UP! I went into the bank today to buy a money order to pay a past due bill when the nice teller said, "Hunt…" (They all know me by name, and at times like this, I wish they didn't), "… Do you know what your balance is?"

"I hoped I was wrong," I answered feeling as small as a 6' 6" guy can feel.

She turned around and printed out something that showed that I was in the hole $236. I was thinking I'm okay because I have a $1000 overdraft protection on the account, until she pulled out another printout which showed that my overdraft was all used up.

I applied the check I was going to use to buy that money order to my account and gave her the little bit of cash I had in my wallet to bring me all the way back up to zero so I could avoid another $26 overdraft charge. On one hand, I was very lucky I happened to go to the bank today so I could avoid another charge I can't afford. On the other hand, is my plane crashing, or does it just look that way?

Okay. That's plenty of conflict and climax for this story. Let's get on with the happy ending!

AUGUST 10, 2007, ANOTHER DREAM: Last night I dreamt that I woke up and walked outside my front door to see that the huge hedge maze, which usually had encompassed my front yard as far as I could see (in that reality), had been mowed down. My first thought was, "Well, life will be simpler now," but then I felt disappointment at seeing all that life removed.

I had thought the dream was purely personal, but the impact of that last phrase in the sentence above just hit me. I think the message of the mowed down maze may have a much more universal message. It seems like a pretty clear illustration of how life will be going to be getting simpler for me and for everyone in the world pretty soon, but that will be accomplished through a great loss.

That being the case, I'm not sure what a happy ending to my own experiences would look like. Maybe this chapter will have to be open until after the ascension. Maybe I'll have to continue it as a running chapter in future books until the happy ending is really obvious to everyone.

AUGUST 12, 2007, THE SECRET: "Ever since we first took on selfish goals and priorities 5000 years ago in Babylon and built that temple to ego, we've been laboring under the illusion that the only essential thing is our own desires and will power. This has made the **one real thing** invisible to us." That's what I said in the *The Lost Art,* and it's key in explaining the misconceptions promoted as ultimate truth by the motivational gurus who wrote that slam dunk success, *The Secret.*

The Secret to life has to do with our harmonious connection to all things. True, we have a lot of power over the events that come into our lives, and people should generally take more responsibility for their own circumstances. However, because of our connection to all things, our own desire and will power are not the only influences in our lives! That would seem fairly intuitive to most people. However, the world of motivational speakers is selling a different theory.

I was in sales for many years, and I appreciate a good pep talk as much as the next guy. However, the authors of this book go so far with their "secret" principle as to say that those who were tortured and murdered in the WW II concentration camps must have set that condition up for themselves. The writers reach this conclusion because they only recognize one principle as the cause of all reality in the world. The problem is that these motivational gurus picked the wrong *one thing* in which to put all their faith.

Speaking biblically, you could say that their teachings promote a false god. They preach that without exception, we personally create everything that happens to us. This exclusive philosophy sets up human ego above the *one* real *thing*. It leads readers away from compassion for others, and thus away from their own heart which would otherwise lead them to knowing the *one* real *thing*. Hearts connect us; egos divide us.

This idea that we personally create **everything** that happens to us by our own thought forms also drives a wedge into unity consciousness. If the only cause in our life is an internal one, who needs everyone else, except, of course, as targets for our marketing campaigns? According to this all-encompassing principle, if we don't meet our quota, the ONLY reason could be that we must not have tried hard enough or held onto the right thought forms tightly enough.

This failure leaves no room for looking for other doors to open, or wondering about the universal plan. We simply failed; and failure, of course, is a bad thing, even though that's how most of us learn best, AND even though learning is the whole point to being on Earth in the first place. The only solution for this detestable failure is to cut ourselves off from any distracting outside influences even more, and get right back out on the streets and sell, sell, sell! Sales managers love this delusion, but it does the rest of us a tremendous disservice.

So…this egotistical "secret" of success cuts us off from our own heart center; it separates us from acknowledgement of our connection to others and how they influence us; and it furthers the illusion of duality by promoting verifiable goal-oriented "success" as the only good influence in our lives.

Years ago, when I was laid off and my marriage fell apart, and I couldn't get a job, and my little bit of life savings all disappeared, my best friends said it was my karma. They said that somehow I must have brought this on myself. Because of their little bit knowledge into how karma and life worked, they had absolutely no compassion for my situation.

That was right before I picked up and moved to the far corner of Montana and resolved to be done with this world as soon as possible. Things got better after my life contract expired, but lately, my life has had some more disappointing surprises. As I look around and see that I'm not alone, I have to wonder what's going on.

The simple answer is that our higher selves are finding a way for many, if not most, of us to face our worst fears in order to help us move past them before this historical human cycle ends. The egotistical illusion that we alone created our present circumstances through our utter failure just adds insult to injury. It totally negates the influence of our connection with an intelligent universe or anyone around us. Personal ego, perspective and preferences are important. But they are by no means *The One Thing*.

As I mentioned a couple days ago, I'm not sure what a happy ending to my predicaments would look like anymore. I'm sure I'll be fine. In fact, I constantly work on happy expectations about the outcome of my situations. However, I don't know what that outcome will be yet because I don't know exactly what Spirit has in mind for me.

There's always more going on than we can possibly know. Things may result in realizing the opposite of my goals (which I work on for about 15 hours every day). That's obviously not my first choice. Yet THE secret is that it doesn't matter!

Our willingness to do the work of the *One Thing*, instead of trying to wield the power of the gods for our own petty preferences, is where the real magic for our future lies. The loving universe won't deny us what we need, but THE secret is learning to work with It, rather trying to control It. Measuring ourselves by how well we attain our personal goals is ONLY the secret to entirely missing the whole point of life.

AUGUST 15, 2007, BRINGING BIG GUNS TO BEAR: Today, I had a meeting of the minds with my higher self. Sure, like most, I send prayers out into the empty air all the time hoping God or someone will answer them. However, for me, until now anyway, it has always taken some serious motivation before I really have the focus to connect with my higher self.

Today, after I withdrew most of my little IRA to temporarily extinguish some financial brush fires, my "What's happening?" cry to the universe was met by my higher self. I never know what obscure little lesson he might feel is worthy of my torment, so I laid down some priorities just as I did before entering this physical life. "Nothing should interfere with my mission." He agreed.

I vowed to listen closely to his guidance and do my best at the tasks in front of me. He answered by filling me with confidence and the strength that comes from knowing that life will be cooperating with me because the big gun himself will be on the front lines clearing the way.

I still don't know what's going to happen, but I do know that my big personal goals are in harmony with what my higher self wants for me during the remainder of this lifetime. I also know that the feeling of confidence and strength I got from that connection today is worth whatever it costs to stay connected!

It's worth giving up my little preferences and comforts if they're deemed not in the highest good or not practically possible. It's also worth whatever time in contemplation it takes every day to reaffirm the compatibility of my goals with the intentions of my higher self.

That superhuman feeling of strength comes and goes. I don't always see through the eyes of my higher self. However, I'm feeling his constant presence these days, along with a growing support system of many guides and loved ones around me.

AUGUST 16, 2007, REALITY CHECK: We channeled yesterday. I asked Billy if maybe there was a hidden purpose to the sudden failure of my business and the utter failure to the business I created to replace my failing business. In looking deeply, my own guides had said that my problems, as well as everyone's right now, are part of the purification we're all going through. The purpose is to help loosen our attachments to things. Putting our attention on more spiritual pursuits helps us, which in turn helps Mother Earth, during this time of transition.

That's all true, but it's also amazing how complicated we make things sometimes. I really like Billy's answer better. He said simply that businesses are failing all over because the economy is not what they portray it to be. He encouraged me to work with the 3D realities I know a little longer, and confirmed my hope for the future in several respects: gamma arrays are causing our vibrations and the vibrations of the Earth to rise. The raising vibrations are causing our DNA to evolve. The new and improved DNA will be making things easier for everyone as soon as they realize their own power. This realization will also facilitate the completion of the shift process.

In the meantime, one possibility I thought of to help get by financially was to start a physic advice service and launch it by posting some of Billy's predictions. I thought maybe we could make a name for ourselves and charge for channelings. Billy said that was fine with him. He told us about a large earthquake which was about to hit Peru. He said it would be a high 7 or low 8 on the Richter scale. I wrote up the prediction, but before I could post it, Danna was led to a site which reported that a 7.9 quake had just hit Peru. Nice call, but it happened too quickly to capitalize on it. Maybe next time.

In that session, Billy also confirmed the happy future of my writing career. So, it seems my world is coming into a new order. It won't be an easily won order, but hard work and discomfort are nothing new.

AUGUST 24, 2007, LIVING THE ALTERNATIVE: I've always seemed to take the "path least travelled." It felt karmic many times. Still, this path has led to some very interesting perspectives. I was lying awake in bed this morning looking at my life from a higher perspective. From there, I could see my main, core life and the major alternatives. As I found myself looking at a very slim possibility of an alternative live, I said to my guide, "But I'm living that life!"

He said, "Yes you are!"

In that instance, I understood the reality of a life without any prearranged contracts. What a mistake it would have been to let my natural inclinations follow my contract and depart from this world a few years ago! I've made my main wishes known and put lots of energy into them, and those bases are well covered. I've been blessed by bonds to loved ones who've been placed in my life for our mutual benefit. I'm writing, which has always been my favourite life's ambition. And I am getting by.

I had hoped to manifest some quick miracles to make my inspirational point to myself and everyone reading this. However, I am doing what I've always wanted and I'm surrounded by loved ones. What more can you really expect in this 3D world? Actually, I do have more. I have the gift of being able to see and know.... My questions somehow puncture the fabric of the unconscious, and I either see the answer myself, or someone from that side tells me.

As I was looking at the slim chance of an alternative life which I'm actually living, I saw ahead a little. When I was looking for my happy ending, I saw it about ten to twelve years out.

However, first I saw it in the eyes of my usually very grounded wife. I see her main life, and I can see the slight chance that love will change that fate. She started living that slight chance after her guides let her meet me a couple years back, when it finally became clear that I wouldn't be checking out anytime soon.

Still, the momentum of life doesn't change on a dime. We both carry our old inertia with us into this brave new world. I can see it changing in both of us. I can see all of our dreams coming true. However, it takes time to manifest everything into physical reality.

This journal has dragged on a lot longer than I anticipated, and like life, it didn't turn out the way I had hoped. However, reality is okay too. We like to give reality a boost with our hopeful expectations, but the fact remains that physical life isn't running solely on all the higher principles yet. It's getting there relatively quickly these days. However, in the meantime, we're getting by with love and the knowledge that our dreams are coming true in ways we could never have even imagined.

Sometimes it seems like the three dimensions of this world must be problems, suffering and change. Yet, even that is changing. Suddenly, we're *looking, seeing and knowing* more all the time. These qualities add dimension to our other three dimensions and are the only real foundation for "happily ever after."

OCTOBER 3, 2007, BAD PLANS: I didn't want to write again until I had an obviously happy ending to report. However, I'm beginning to think the deliverance of that sort of inspiration may be someone else's job. I'm writing about what I see and know. Hopefully, the message that evolves will be that it's safe to look closely at reality even when it's not shaping up the way we had planned. I've always believed that it's okay to take our eyes off the goal long enough to see what's really going on.

Yesterday, I got an interesting perspective where I saw the original order to my life. I saw the reason for my early exit plan, and knew that it was a good plan. Still, here I am. My higher self has surrounded me with loved ones from my past as a way to build a new life. I'm blessed with the opportunity to show love to them by taking care of them. However yesterday, I found myself entirely depleted. To make a long story short, desperation once again made a connection between me and my higher self.

I asked if it was alright if I just came home. He said, "Fine."

Then, hours later, I said, "I don't mind sticking around to do the job, but you've got to help make that job possible."

He said, "Okay."

What you have to understand is that when my higher self speaks, it's not like hearing anyone else. When, he said, "Okay," that reply filled the heavens and reached into the darkest places of my mind and soul. I felt we had an agreement on August 15th, when we had our last meeting of the minds, but I evidently needed reassurance. Things haven't felt like they were going right. I know it's been my fault, but that doesn't make any better.

My own guides told me a while back that my life was a reflection of my own wishes, and they showed me how I sabotaged myself. I had made it known that I wanted my business to wind down so I could write full time, and that wish was granted. However, since that plan was initiated without any prelife contract or any other divine intervention, it was a little flawed. My business was winding down all right, and I was writing. However, the detail of money had been left out of the plan.

About a month ago when they brought this to my attention, I put out a new prayer for the revitalization of my business until my writing begins to pay off. Receivables have more than doubled, and that's a good sign of the developing new order. However, the problem which developed in the last year over this little oversight has gotten pretty overwhelming.

At any rate, that's what led to my second plea for help from my higher self yesterday, and I went to bed feeling that my renewed contract with life has a much better chance of getting on target now. Then, last night I had a dream where I met up with a lot of the most important guys from the different eras of my life all in one room.

One uniquely quirky guy just strolled up to the door. One quiet guy I've always wanted to know better showed up on a huge, rumbling, magnificent motorcycle. There were probably a dozen men all together, and I had time with them all, one on one. I also got to see how well that diverse crowd got along together.

It felt like a real gift! Accomplishing that reunion in the dream state is also one more reason for me not to go home anytime soon. That experience will hold me for a while now.

Incidentally, the job I see myself here to do isn't changing the world or saving the planet. I'd be delighted if it turned out that I had a hand in those things in some small way. However, my personal goals are really simple. I just want to take care of my responsibilities—like everyone else. I want to see my two little girls safely through all the emotional and physical changes that lie ahead as they bloom into adulthood, and as our planet does the same. True, I may have some unusual interests, memories, observations, and thoughts... but, other than that, I'm just an average guy trying to get by.

OCTOBER 5, 2007, POST TRILOGY LETDOWN: A year ago, I had two reasons for staying in this world: One was to take care of my two little girls. The other was to try to make sense out of a life which felt all wrong.

Everything I came up with fell short of explaining what had happened to my life and why. Then, a year ago, when I met Danna, I suddenly started getting answers though channeling and through a better connection with my own guides which resulted from that channeling. In that time, I revised my first book, *The BIG Fake-out*. I also researched and wrote, *The Don Q Point of View*, a book that explores a particularly peculiar past life. As I got even more answers, I wrote, this book, and I've just finished it. That's three books written and. to date, zero published.

I've gotten all the answers I was looking for. Now, having satisfied this curiosity, one of my two reasons for staying in this world is suddenly gone!

My life hasn't improved in any noticeable way. If anything, it's gotten more challenging and less efficient. I went to work yesterday as a high school substitute teacher for $7 per hour. While I was gone, I missed an order for which the customer found another supplier before I could get back to her.

Anyway, it's hard to know where my time and effort is best spent. I scramble constantly to make things better, and they only seem to be getting worse. I started to subdivide some land when prices were good only to have them drop to about half before the subdivision process was complete. Now I have lots of subdivision costs I can't pay, and I can't afford to finish the process until I sell the lot. I started a new business to replace the failing one, but $20,000 later, that business has yet to result in one order.

I don't mean to whine, but I am still feeling the effects of a life without any prearranged set-ups. I used Free Will to change the conditions that set up my contracted early exit, and I've recently been given all my answers. Those are both really big blessings!

Yet, they're blessings which have resulted in a profound depression. After researching, analyzing and exploring all my answers and detailing them into three books, artifacts I can put them on a shelf and take them down now and then to review, I'm left with one question: "What about my REAL life?!"

Still, when I get a grip, one biggie jumps out at me. All these experiences and ALL the answers came in the last year. I feel a little like Scrooge: "The spirits did it all in one night!"

Even if that is enough time to unlock the secrets of the universe, maybe it's not enough time to inject an empty life with meaning and success. Maybe I should give the universe a little more time to work the kinks out of my life. I'm sure if I asked the question of my guides, they'd say I need a little more patience and a little more focus on the *one thing*.

Another thing I noticed over the last few days is how many concerned beings from the other side have been trying to help me. They leave me alone most of the time, but the last couple days, I felt their presence strongly. I was getting a lot of advice like, "Take it easy," "take a long, hot shower," "exercise," "go outside and walk…" I followed all the advice and snapped out of it much quicker than ever before.

Then, as I became resolved with reality as it is here and now, my attention floated back to the running guidance on magic, which I combined into the ending of chapter six. The magic really flowed when I wrote that chapter! I KNOW the answers! I guess I better just go back and sit in my own class and practice the lessons a little longer.

NOVEMBER 10, 2007, "MAKE THE MAGIC!" Today, the kids are gone and since it's a weekend, I don't have much work to do. All is quiet, and I'd really like to feel the inspiration which comes with channeling. However, now that my writing projects are complete, I don't have any important questions anymore. As I pondered what I should ask, this message came through: "Instead of asking questions, make magic today!"

With that message came the vision of sitting at the center of the universe with people and situations spinning around me. These people and plans come into harmony with me and add to the loving core of everything or they eventually fly off. I don't pursue the ones which look good, nor do I fear the ones which don't, because nothing can change the center of the universe.

It's a very comfortable spot sitting with all that's real at the center of all the action. It's reassuring looking on as the gravity of that situation makes all the magic. Seeing my oneness with that one indestructible, magical core fills me with peace. Suddenly, I've been pulled away from life's scattered activities and human hopes, and renewed with the knowledge of my place at the core of it all. That core is rock solid, and finally my answers outweigh the questions.

NOVEMBER 14, 2007, THE DEVELOPING ANSWERS: I was really referring above to the big questions like how to have faith in the order of the universe and our purpose in it—stuff like that. However, as far as the details of my own life, the mess I've made seems to be falling into a new order too. Regarding the supplier problem I mentioned in one of my first entries to this journal, I wrote a couple of killer letters detailing the extent of the damage their breach of contract caused me. The first letter went to the supplier, and the next one went to their attorney. I never heard back after writing their attorney, but I did stop getting collection calls and notices, so we seem to have an understanding.

Also, the last time we channeled, a couple weeks ago, Billy talked about the "law of silence." He said that showing anyone what I write or telling them about it before I'm done will break the bubble of magic in which I sit.

The "law of silence," makes life more graceful and activates the patience and faith that's necessary for magic to actually manifest in this world. I never said that in my chapters on magic, but I'm saying it now, and I'm feeling how that works now. Better late than never—says the guy who only really got it together after his life contract on this Earth had expired.

NOVEMBER 30, 2007, HAPPILY EVER AFTER: I'm not waiting to be happy with life anymore! I've always found myself waiting and wishing to run smack into the realization of my dreams, and that realization always seems to be lurking tauntingly close, right around the next corner. These expectations have suckered me into waiting for things (the wrong thing) to set me free my entire life!

First it was a car, then a wife, then a house, then a better wife, then a better house… There's always something wrong with physical life. Yet, if there were a lot less wrong with my life, I might miss the point entirely that it's important to be satisfied with things as they are.

So, I sit back down in magic school just in time to hear the conclusion:

> *So, be the magic latent in every situation which is just waiting to resolve. Keep the center of yourself solid by being there. Don't chase the objects of your desire away from that center. Let them come to you.*
>
> *Feel the living, nurturing universe all around you. Be aware of the help your loved ones, physically deceased or living, are always giving you. Their love creates its own magic and swirls around you and your affairs at all times. You don't really NEED anything else!*
>
> *Draw on it. Be the miracle others are waiting for. Carry the magic with you at all times in all situations, so you aren't dependant on anything or anyone. Remember, you are only dependant on the loving universe, and that magic is always with you.*

With that, class was dismissed, and my guide whispered in my ear, "That was your final lesson."

That could be my final lesson for now, but that lesson is far from over! I know that because I've heard those words before. The last time was when I was twelve. All my questions had been answered through nightly trips with my guide to wisdom temples. After telling me that my lessons were finished, my guide, Rebazar, told me that I'd spend the rest of my life really learning what I had been taught. Now, that I've just received another "final" lesson, I know the same is true. Learning to "be the magic" is a life long pursuit, and life is infinite.

I've made some headway toward realizing some of my personal goals. I'm learning a happy appreciation for the nurturing nature of life. I'm feeling the source of all magic securely in my own core through my connection to Nature, and I'm learning the power of patience—all things I wouldn't have discovered if everything I wanted came easily.

After years of resenting all those around me who operate on automatic by simply following their contracted path, I'm finally coming into harmony with a new contract of my own. I'm a writer now, and my simple plan is to graciously accept what I have to do while I keep on writing. I have an understanding with my higher self, and I feel life falling into place. So, my story may not *end* happily ever after, but comfortable in my resolve, it's going to *continue* happier than ever, ever after.

JANUARY 21, 2008, THE MATRIX: By the way, I discovered that the publisher I mentioned earlier which I saw had an interest in my first manuscript was never even sent a proposal by my agent. When I noticed this after my contract with that agent was up, I quickly filled out the publisher's form, and sent them my manuscript priority mail. They couldn't have had it more than two days when I got a call. I talked to the publisher for almost an hour during which time she told me that they would be taking my manuscript into the acquisition meeting the next day. Geeze—it made me wonder how long they were waiting for it. I thought it was a shoe-in, but weeks later, it was finally rejected. My vision was true. That publisher was greatly interested in my manuscript, but my assumption of publication was wrong.

At any rate, I continue editing everything I've written, and what a blessing that has been! What has hit me repeatedly as I reread my writing is that even though I've been given answers, I still have trouble actually internalizing them. I've had the same lack of faith problems over and over. Each time I'd come to one of the many places in this book that explains the reason for faith, it was like finding it anew. I was inspired and reassured just like a first time reader might be. I suppose that's because I just haven't been totally convinced. Also, it looks now like that lack of faith made a real difference in my life.

I was reassured through channeled answers many times, and by two different entities, that my first two books would get published within a given timeframe. I believed them, but when my business went down, and the business I created to replace it failed, I got depressed. Now, both these entities have told me that my lack of faith changed my future. The time period in which I was supposed to get published came and went. I've had to regroup and maintain a strong confidence in my writing much longer than is natural for me. In fact, I'm still working hard on coming into harmony with that success.

Most people never really see what causes the circumstances in their lives. We assume it's our actions, which affect everything and that our personal worry is our own business and has no effect on the outside world. In actuality, there is no "outside world." There's just one world, and we create our place in it by our every thought, feeling and reaction.

"Knowing the truth is not the same thing as living the truth." Morpheous said that in *The Matrix* to explain the limitations of everyone except "The One."

"The One" Morpheous referred to was supposed to be endowed with so much more faith in what everyone knew about the state of their being that he was to be their savior. That's a great story for illustrating the power of faith! Unfortunately, it fosters the belief and hope that someone else might come along and provide a quick answer to the dilemma of our existence. We each have our own path and, in the real world, no one can make up for our own lack of faith. We each have to take responsibility for being our own saviors.

After going over what I KNOW many times, and still being vulnerable to doubt, I'm getting really serious about turning that around. I'm looking closely now at the causal relationships I've found. I'm trying to see how things work so I can believe in those workings.

In the chapter entitled "The Lost Art," I wrote: "…Nature, that living *matrix,* which molds all creation. According to Webster, a matrix is 'the womb; the cavity where anything is formed; a mold.'"

Material that goes into a mold and allowed time to cure will always come out with the desired result. It's a law of nature! Imagining our thoughts making molds for the physical world may seem magical sometimes. It may be hard to believe that putting the scrap from our lives into these molds will make a perfect sculpture. But believe it. Thoughts are what make up the molds, which shape whatever we put into them.

That's the truth. I could write forever rehashing that. I've already spent many lifetimes relearning it! It's time to just focus on it, *see* it, and *know* that I know it.

Okay, Hunt. This is it! Live it! If you don't, no one is going to do it for you. Face it: In this movie, YOU are *The One*!

JULY 28, 2008, ONE YEAR LATER: It's been about a year since I described my challenges: 3 credit cards, all at or above their limits, an overdrawn checking account and an overdrawn overdraft account; no money for the mortgage, the need to put about $25,000 into a road so I could finish the subdivision process, and advertising expenses of about $20,000 for new products which never resulted in a single sale. I think that about covers it.

In the last year since I started writing this journal, **all these problems have miraculously disappeared.** I was really hoping I was going to be able to say that!

Business picked up some, and there was a stock I bought with money I skimmed off my home construction loan, which I'd forgotten about because it was preferred stock that I couldn't sell for two years and because it had dropped in price whenever I checked it. To make a long story short, when I could finally sell it, it miraculously (I love that word!) went up from 12 cents to $2.00 in less than two weeks. Also, it was just the right two-week period because I was going to sell as soon as I could anyway! As it turned out, my initial $5000 (which I had all but written off) turned into about $20,000 in the two years I owned it.

I put money into the road construction so I could begin the subdivision process, and paid off all three credit cards. I got the best deal in town on the road with what everyone said was the best company in town for the job, but when a lot more work was suddenly necessary, I had to agree to pay on a time and materials basis. Just then, my neighbor, who had never done any major work to his property in the seven years I've lived here, decided to dig a humongous pond. Suddenly, we came into a lot of free dirt. They've been trucking it out of there constantly for four days now. I also only have to pay to move it a few hundred yards instead of a many miles. They estimate that with all that free dirt and what I'm saving in trucking it I'm going to save about $6,000!

The lot has never sold, and I'm not entirely out of the woods financially yet. Still, after what's happened this last year, I'm sure I soon will be. I finally got one book publication offer from a traditional publisher, but they wanted me to buy a slug of books, so I'm just going to self-publish.

I've spent the last year (while I was trying to get published) greatly improving all three books. I have an actual copy of my first book in hand now, and the other two should be coming out soon. I was just doing one final check of this one when I decided to make one last entry—to tell you how MIRACULOUS things have turned out. It really is a magical universe!

Bibliography

Melchizedek, Drunvalo. *The Ancient Secret of the Flower of Life, Volume 1.* Arizona: Light Technology Publishing, 1998. pp. 101- 116, 161-169.

Melchizedek, Drunvalo. *The Ancient Secret of the Flower of Life, Volume 2.* Arizona: Light Technology Publishing, 2000. pp 429—437, 440 -454.

Braden, Gregg. *Awakening to Zero Point, The Collective Initiation,* Washington: Radio Bookstore Press, 1997. pp vi—viii, 4—6, 19-21, 28-35, 40-47, 81, 102.

Sitchin, Zecharia. *The 12th Planet.* New York: Stein and Day / Publishers, 1976. pp 292-343, 350.

Doreal, M. *The Emerald Tablets of Thoth—The Atlantean,* Nashville, TN: Source Books, Inc., 1994.

Printed in the United States
147790LV00003B/2/P

LOOKING, SEEING AND KNOWING

Dear Suzy,

Thank you for the nice comment & all of your support!

B [signature]